WITHDRAWN

The
Richest
Lady In
Town

The Richest Lady In Town

Joyce Landorf

ZONDERVAN PUBLISHING HOUSE
OF THE ZONDERVAN CORPORATION
GRAND RAPIDS, MICHIGAN 49506

If not otherwise indicated, Scripture quotations are from the King James Bible.

Grateful acknowledgment is expressed to the publishers for permission to quote from the following Bible translations:

The Living Bible, copyright © 1971 by Tyndale House Publishers.

The New Testament: A Translation in the Language of the People, by Charles B. Williams. Copyright © 1937 by Bruce Humphries, Inc., copyright © renewed 1965 by Edith S. Williams. Published by Moody Press.

The New Testament in Modern English. Copyright © 1958 by J. B. Phillips. Published by The Macmillan Company.

The New Testament in the Translation of Monsignor Ronald Knox. Copyright © 1944 by Sheed and Ward, Inc., New York.

The Revised Standard Version of the Bible. Copyright © 1952 by The Division of Christian Education of the National Council of the Churches of Christ in the United States of America.

Weymouth's New Testament in Modern Speech, by Richard Francis Weymouth, as revised by J. A. Robertson. Published by special arrangement with James Clarke and Company Ltd., London, by Harper and Row Publishers.

THE RICHEST LADY IN TOWN
Copyright © 1973 by The Zondervan Corporation
Grand Rapids, Michigan

Thirteenth printing   May 1976

Library of Congress Catalog Card Number 72-95523

Library of Congress Cataloging in Publication Data

Landorf, Joyce.
   The richest lady in town.

   1. Christian life — 1960-   2. Landorf, Joyce.
I. Title.
BV4501.2.L3183   248'.4   73-500

Printed in the United States of America

*This book is gratefully dedicated to two rewarding
investments my husband and I have made.
We've been drawing on one for nineteen years
and on the other for seventeen years.
They have returned greater gains than
any other investment on the market.
We are independently wealthy, more than we ever
dreamed possible, because of them — our children*

RICK AND LAURIE

Acknowledgments

To these rich ladies, my creditors, my debt of thanks.

Pris Norton, who pushed her way through our crowded Sunday school class to ask, "Joyce, the Lord has really laid you on my heart. Can I be of any help? Could I type a rough draft or something?"

Virginia Smith, who took time off from being a wife, mother and registered nurse to give my manuscript a critic's evaluation and said revealing things like, "Joyce, you've said the same thing three times on one page. I *like* what you're saying, in fact it's the message of the entire book, but rework it and say it *once* so it has more impact!"

Clare Bauer, who phoned long distance and usually just asked with patient love, "Joyce, haven't you finished it yet?"

And last, but not at all least, Sheila Rapp, who didn't say anything at all. She simply put her husband, children and house into "planned neglect" and typed up a perfect master copy *with carbons.*

Contents

The Richest Lady in Town!

The Richest Lady in Town!

A millionaire lives on my street, and would you believe it — it's me! Oh, you'll never catch me strutting about in a mink-lined pantsuit, and you'll never see me driving around in a pale lavender Rolls Royce. In fact, I rarely talk about my wealth, but *I am* a bona fide, honest-to-goodness, real live heiress.

I don't have my millions tied up in trust funds, mutual funds, or future funds. I have all of it right here and now. Personally, I don't care for people who are always bragging about money. That's why I've never felt I should say too much about it. But an awful thought hit me yesterday. *Maybe there are a lot of people wandering about who haven't heard of their inheritance.* I certainly didn't know about mine for a long time. Actually some years back I suspected that I had come into a fortune, but I wasn't really positive until I received official notification one Thanksgiving day seven years ago.

That day started out like any other "big dinner" day. Lots of cooking, cleaning, and shopping, lots of thinking, planning, and creating went ahead of the day, because I wanted it to be special.

11

My table looked like a fold-out page from the *Better Homes and Gardens* food section. The gold and white chrysanthemums with tall, tapered yellow candles, gleaming white china, and polished silver was the perfect setting for the dear people who sat down to "ooh" and "ahh" appropriately — my mother, father, sister, grandparents, husband Dick, and our children, Laurie and Rick. They had never looked so beautiful. It was an unusual dinner from the start because I had never had exactly that combination of family before; and since both my mother and grandfather died within nine months of that dinner, I was never to have that blending of people again.

Dick asked my grandfather to pray the blessing for the food, and in the good old Hungarian tradition grandpa pushed his chair back, stood up, began "Dear Lord" in English, faltered a bit, and switched to Hungarian. I understood some of what he said, but my children didn't. It never mattered. His prayer made us all know *God was listening*, and we felt shivers run up our spines. After his "Amen" grandma added her benediction of "Hallelujah," and we were ready to eat. (Actually, they were ready to eat — I was still back on the prayer because I knew grandpa had asked the Lord to "Bless the hands that lovingly prepared this.")

The dinner, in my book, was a culinary delight — a smashing gourmet occasion. And it was a success with everyone except grandma. She could cook circles around me, and she had little use for a dinner that didn't start out with beef or chicken soup (complete with those little farina dumplings), Hungarian chicken paprikas, and two other meat dishes (with hand-made noodles this time), and ending up with her *rétes* and strudel (dainty, tissue-paper-thin dough surrounding apples, cinnamon, and nuts). My baked acorn squash with its buttery pecan syrup sauce didn't sit very *Hungarian* with her, but she was a good sport and picked her way around it. She probably went home and cooked up a batch of food for grandpa to make up for my American-style feast.

I don't recall too much of the conversation that glorious day other than that we laughed a great deal, and the dinner time was stretched into two-and-a-half noisy, wonderful hours.

It was after the last piece of pumpkin pie had disappeared, while I was cleaning the last bit of spilled gravy off my white tiled sink that I was alone with Dick. He had moved my mother and grandma out of the kitchen into the living room and was carefully fitting the leftover turkey into our overcrowded refrigerator when we got the great news!

My grandfather had vanished from view right after dinner and without my knowledge had taken his own personal tour of our house, garage, and backyard, ending up in the kitchen with his arms folded over his fat tummy and a contented smile on his face.

"Dick, you know vat?" he said in his fractured English.

Dick shut a cupboard door and gave grandpa his undivided attention. "What, grandpa?"

"Dick, you are millionaire!"

There was a small, protesting laugh out of Dick, and he patted grandpa's shoulder and mumbled some-

13

thing about that not being true. He intended to end grandpa's conversation, but grandpa had given his speech considerable thought and was not about to be shushed.

So grandpa straightened to his full height and said, "You listen, Dick. I tell you trute. You are big millionaire. You got this house, you got children, you got big backyard, you got her (pointing at me), she got you." His finger was right under Dick's nose. "And you know *vat else?*" He was speaking quite loudly because he didn't want either of us to miss the punch line. "You millionaires! *You got God!*"

Since both of us instantly remembered that only a few years before we had had no real home, no love for each other or children, and had come so very close to succeeding in taking our lives, the ringing truth clanged loudly enough to nearly deafen us. We were absolutely stunned at the incredible news. How would you feel after being told you had come into a huge fortune? For a few moments we just stood there.

Then Dick put his arms around dear, wise, old grandpa and said in a loving tone, "You're right, grandpa. You're right!"

It was a year later that I began the first draft of the book *His Stubborn Love* — the story of the making of a millionaire. Months after grandpa died, I remembered his clearly stated words, "You are millionaires!"

You see, I *am* the richest lady in town, not because of hoarded cash, immense investments in stocks and bonds, an heirloom collection of jewelry, or vast property holdings, but because of God's outpouring of spiritual wealth. I have, at my fingertips, large

14

holdings of spiritual gifts, treasures, and yes, even power working and readily available in me. You do, too, if you belong to Christ. In fact, we have "far more than we would ever dare to ask or even dream of — infinitely beyond our highest prayers, desires, thoughts, or hopes!" (Eph. 3:20, *Living Bible*).

So, come on, leave whatever you're doing and go to the bank with me. I know the folks at the bank and I'll introduce you to everyone. After that, I'll sign you into the safe deposit area and together we will peek into the box of treasured riches! Some of the greatest values are found in the "Talent Account" (it always surprises me); the "Gentleness Account" (it continues to cool the hot, flaring temperatures of today's crisis living); the "Opportunity Account" (it gives me a direct connection with the Man at the top — the very top!); and the "Refinement Account" (I'd *rather* do without this one, yet each time I draw on it I wouldn't take a million dollars for the experience) — these and other accounts are all available to you. They are at your fingertips, ready and waiting for you to do your own taking.

What's that? You don't think you've got any such accounts? Oh, yes, you do — it's probably just that no one has ever pointed out your bonanza of wealth. In fact, you may have *more* than I do, which is just fine with me, but what a shame it would be to live your life without the knowledge of your legacy!

You'd be like the people we read about in the newspapers every now and then. "Older woman dies of starvation. One hundred thousand dollars found under her mattress." "Man dies in filth and squalor of tenement building. Fifty thousand dollars and stocks totaling a half million found in kitchen drawer."

That's a preposterous situation! Yet almost every day I meet Christians who are convinced they are destitute and penniless, when in reality they are wealthy.

Just a couple of weeks ago as I sat in the dentist's chair waiting for the final numbness to set in, the dental assistant asked me what I was writing. (Now, that's a dangerous question to ask a writer because it really turns on the flow of words.) So I began to tell her about this book and I said, "You know, even though you are a young widow with five children, Diane, you are wealthy because you are God's woman with an immense inheritance."

Her eyes filled with tears, and she said, "Oh, Joyce, I needed to be reminded of that. I'm so bogged down with the problems of living that I had forgotten how *very* rich I am!" Then she spent a few more minutes encouraging me to finish this book quickly.

If you are a Christian and you truly don't feel wealthy, try reading Ephesians 1. It tells of our inheritance. Phrases like, "In Him too we have been made heirs" (v. 11, Weymouth's translation); "stamped with the promised Holy Spirit as a guarantee of purchase" (v. 13, Phillips' translation); the Holy Spirit "is the first installment of our inheritance" (v. 14, Williams' translation) show that you are wealthy whether you feel like it or not.

This book has not been written to tell you how I *found* my first million before forty years of age, but rather, how I've learned to *spend* it! Read on!

The Talent Account

The Talent Account

The first account I'd like you to see is a large one called "Talent." And before you skip lightly through it thinking, "This account is not for me because I have no talent," let me tell you of an experience I had a few months ago. I was singing and speaking for the Protestant Women of the Chapel at an Army base in Okinawa.

At the beginning of my program, I said that when I finished singing I would be speaking on talent. I felt someone, perhaps many, would hear the word "talent" and think, *Well, that lets me out — I'm not talented at all!*

I was counting on the Lord to really speak through me since many women have the problem of a low estimate of self-worth.

One of the first women to reach me after the meeting was a lovely lady whose eyes were sparkling and glistening with tears.

"You know, Joyce," she began, "when you said you'd be talking about talent today, I almost got up and walked out because if there is one thing I don't have, it's that. But I stayed anyway. I'm so glad I did, because as you spoke, God pointed out one talent after another in my life. I had no idea they existed. I was deeply moved and convicted. I've asked the Lord to forgive me for not recognizing them, and I've come out of this meeting feeling useful and knowing I'm needed. I'm looking forward to fulfilling some life goals."

She was not the only woman who came to the meeting feeling inadequate and untalented. Many women honestly believe they have *no* God-given talent and, what's worse, no self-worth.

A minister recently told me that 50 percent of the women he counseled in his office were there because of their feelings of having no worth, no talent, and no real purpose in living.

The woman in Okinawa who spoke to me had fallen into the common trap of defining talent as *only* the ability to play the piano, to sing, or to paint lovely oil paintings, when in reality, talent is having a natural, God-given ability to do something, *anything*, well.

You might ask, "Great, what are the 'somethings I do very well' in *my* life?"

Here is a list of examples:

1. The talent to be cheerful — particularly when nothing is going right, you've spent the day chasing all over town, and everyone has been less than nice.

2. The talent to be hospitable — to open your home and entertain angels (or teenagers) even though your couch is threadbare, the living room needs painting, or you just began payments on a white shag carpet.

20

3. The talent to know how to make your husband feel like he's the handsomest, wisest, smartest man in town, even though *you,* more than anyone alive, know all his weaknesses and faults.

4. The talent to speak with loving tact. I know a woman who, if she wanted to, could give you a "bawling out" with such tact you wouldn't realize it until three weeks later. That's real talent!

5. The talent to take a course in oil painting, sewing, or business and *finish* it. That requires the talent of self-discipline!

6. The talent to upholster your own chair, add unique buttons to a ready-made dress, or take a jiffy pattern and make baby sacques for the missionary project even though sewing a straight seam has never been your strong point.

7. The talent of being on time. Now here's a talent that's rare today.

8. The talent of communicating love *without* words — by a look, a pat on the arm, a smile, or just taking the *time* to look at a child's drawing.

9. The talent of finding out what "pleasures" each member of your family and *doing it* on a regular basis. In our family, Rick loves smashing, large breakfasts, Laurie adores onion soup, and Dick thinks I should ride *with* him on our Honda 90, so I do them all regularly. It's a beautiful thing to pleasure those you love.

10. The talent of listening when someone speaks. An astonishing number of people never heard of this talent, but once you find a friend talented in this di-

rection you never get over it! You stand in awe and your love for him deepens.

11. The talent of watching how your children throw down their school books and asking God's wisdom in wisely asking, "Hi, how was school today?"

12. The talent to make lumpless gravy like my mother-in-law does.

These are twelve talents that popped into my mind as I sat writing. There are many, many more. Did you find one of yours? If not, make your own list. The talents are endless. Let's go back for a moment to the first talent, the talent of being cheerful.

It's easy to be cheerful and kind to lovely, easy-to-get-along-with people, but if God has given you this talent, you'll have high adventure just on an average day of shopping, banking, and running errands. The opportunities to be cheerful are endless!

The big joy of this talent is the powerful witness it gives.

For three years now I have been actively engaged in presenting Christ to two checkers and three box boys at the supermarket and three or four tellers at the bank. I pray for them regularly and dearly covet their souls for God — though some of them have no idea that for years their names have been on my daily prayer list. Each time I am with them I witness, smile, and listen very carefully (not necessarily in that order), and God has produced some special miracles in several lives. Now it's true, He used my first book in one case, but other than that, my singing and piano-playing talents were not called upon. In fact, never once during these three years of shopping or banking have I wheeled in my piano and said, "Have I got a treat for you! I'm going to use the piano talent God has given to me as a witness to you." Nor have I jumped up on the checkout counter to sing a few numbers and *use my talents!* In fact, some of the very ones who were reached this year have *never* heard me sing, and it's quite conceivable they will never know of those talents.

The talents they *have* seen are of a quite different nature. These other talents begin with coming up to the checkout counter at the supermarket and beating the checker at saying, "Hi, how are you today?" She's paid to be polite — I'm not.

One day at the bank, after I said "Hello, how are you today?" the teller put down her pencil, shook her head, and said, "Joyce, you are something else! You aren't like any other Christian I've ever known."

I wasn't sure exactly how to take that, so I asked, "How do you mean?"

"You always radiate" (she stumbled for words here because she was in unfamiliar territory) "uh, Christian love. If I didn't know you were religious I would never have guessed you to be a Christian. You're cheerful, kind, and have a sense of humor."

"You mean other Christians don't?" I asked.

"Not when they come in here," she snapped.

What a sad commentary on fellow Christians!

The talent for being cheerful, smiling, and pleasant even when it's raining buckets of problems is the talent Paul and Silas had — particularly when they *sang* in

23

prison! It was a God-given ability that had them singing in spite of everything.

It's highly possible that, if your talent is being cheerful or one of the others on my list, you will never become famous. Books may not be written about your life, songs may never be sung or dedicated to you, but the God who sees and knows all things keeps perfect records. He does not classify your special ability of being a great cook, knowing how to bake apricot pie, balancing the checkbook, dressing a skinned knee, raising, teaching, and training children, being a librarian, secretary, or clerk as non-talents.

On the contrary, through Paul we have these words, "I can never stop thanking God for all the wonderful gifts he has given you, now that you are Christ's: he has enriched your whole life. . . . Now you have every grace and blessing; every spiritual gift and power for doing his will are yours during this time of waiting for the return of our Lord Jesus Christ" (1 Cor. 1:4, 5, 7, *Living Bible*).

We tend to get all hung up with our preconceived ideas as to which talents are really important, and in the confusion we miss God's plan for our lives.

Not long ago someone asked our son Rick, "How does it feel to have such a beautiful and talented mother?"

He answered matter-of-factly, "Just great, but you should taste her chicken and dumplings."

I really appreciated his answer, partly because the "talent" of making chicken and dumplings came *after* long practice, but mainly because it told me that in

24

his mind the cooking talent was just as great as, if not greater than, my singing.

Perhaps you can't possibly think of cooking chicken and dumplings as a talent. However, I think it takes enormous talent to be a wife and mother today. If it doesn't, why are one out of every two marriages ending in divorce? If it takes no talent to bake a great pie, why is it so many homes and restaurants serve such inferior pies — or none at all? If it doesn't take talent to raise children, how come juvenile crime rates are spiraling upward? If it doesn't take talent to be a Sunday school teacher, why does the super-intendent keep pleading for more workers all the time?

Yes, I *am* oversimplifying it a bit, but you do get the message, don't you? It takes *talent* to do even ordinary tasks expertly.

Think about your own life for a moment. Isn't there something special you do that certainly could be listed as a talent?

After hearing me say this the other day, a friend of mine nodded her head knowingly and said, "Let me tell you, the mother who just listens to her child practicing the piano and is able to keep her sanity and sense of humor is displaying a great deal of God-given talent!"

I can still picture another woman who said to me, "Oh, sure you *know* what talents He's given you, but He's never told me what mine are and I'm fifty-one years old, so it's a little late to find out."

"Are you married?" I asked.

"Yes," she answered.

25

"Any children?"

"Yes, eight." She said that quite nonchalantly.

I asked her to tell me about them.

"They are all marvelous kids," she said. "Some married, some have gone into medicine, some are ministers, and one is a missionary."

It was incredible. There she stood, saying in effect, "Poor me, I don't have any talents," when she had produced eight fabulous, worthwhile human beings who were living out God's plan!

I blurted out, "Don't tell me that didn't take talent — or did your kids just grow up like weeds without water or cultivation? Didn't you feed and clothe them physically, mentally, and spiritually? Didn't you spank and correct them? Didn't you give them praise, love, and the benefit of God's wisdom? Didn't you pay for voice, piano, and clarinet lessons? Isn't all that being a 'professional mother' just as in my singing and playing I am called a 'professional musician'?" Who dares say that doesn't take talent?

I pray that you will allow God to open your eyes to the unique talents He's given you for the world in which you live. You may not be rich in *my* talents, but I'm not rich in yours either. All talents are from God. It's what you do with them that really makes them worthwhile.

Do you remember the little boy who gave Jesus his lunch of five loaves and two fishes? It was hardly enough to feed himself and a friend, much less the thousands who were there that day, yet *he gave what he had.* From that point — the point of surrendering what he had — Jesus did the rest!

Don't sit back in the comfort of a rut and say you have no talent; rather ask God to use what you've already got, to make you vitally aware of the special abilities He may choose to develop.

Now, let's say that in these past moments God has truly revealed some of the areas in your life where you do have special abilities. How do you handle it? Do you become super-conceited or piously humble? What should your attitude be?

The key that really opens up the Talent Account is an unlikely one found in the Beatitudes.

I had never looked at the Beatitudes and thought about my own connection to them until I read a marvelous piece of writing called *The Beatitudes for Women* by my friend, Colleen Evans. * I sang and spoke at the First Presbyterian Church of La Jolla, California, where Colleen's husband is pastor. At each plate was a copy of her *Beatitudes*. It gave me a glimpse of an account loaded with resources, so I began to study seriously those remarkable words of Jesus.

The Beatitude that grabbed my heart as far as talent is concerned was the one about being humble. Phillips' translation says: "How happy are the humble-minded." No other word in Christian circles is so battered and misused as "humble." Sermons about it go from one extreme to another. One preacher stresses we are all "worm-like" and totally unworthy. The next preacher tells us we are *powerful*, "we can do all things." I got tired of wondering just how to be balanced in being

* Colleen Evans has since expanded her thoughts in the book *A New Joy.*

27

humble, so I began searching the scriptures for the guidelines God has given us.

Unfortunately, the word "humble" is often linked with having talent. It's almost as though, if you don't have talent, then humility is not one of your problems. But we all need humility in our lives; it acts like a lens to bring things into proper focus.

As Colleen Evans says: "She is a happy woman who knows that without God she is *nothing! But with God* she has great potential and strength!"

You don't have to have an inferiority complex. You don't have to sing out the words to that old hymn ". . . for such a worm as I. . . ." Listen, God paid a fantastic price for you, though as a matter of fact, He doesn't owe you a thing! He could have left you stumbling around, wading through one problem after another, living one horrible, unjust day after another, but by God's great, stubborn love, He has *chosen* to care — to buy back, to give Himself to you. He's also given each of us *talents!*

I know perfectly well that God has given me the ability to sing; and I know equally well I have *no* talent at fixing my own hair. I know, too, that I can cook Hungarian stuffed cabbages *(Töltö Kaposzta)* to perfection and that I have mastered three chords on the guitar, though a fourth won't come through my fingers no matter how hard I practice. What am I saying? Just this: I know my abilities and I know my limitations. The moment I confuse or distort these facts, humility goes out the window.

The first time I sang a solo in a large church on the West Coast, I was thirteen years old. I did, as my mother succinctly put it, "a good job" and after the service three older ladies approached me. One said, "My dear" (right there was my first clue — I knew I was going to get it). They didn't say anything about the song or my rendition. They said just this: "We are going to pray God keeps you humble."

That is the greatest left-handed compliment in the world. It lifts you up and slaps you down in one short sentence. Those ladies put me into the position of almost having to apologize for my talent. From then on, when people did thank me for my singing, I'd say, "Oh, I can't sing, really I have so much to learn, etc., etc.," hoping they'd think I was humble.

It wasn't until after I became a Christian that I could honestly face the fact that God had given me a voice and some people, upon hearing it, heard the Lord speaking. When they complimented me, I could honestly say, "Thank you, isn't the Lord marvelous!" Without Him I'm nothing, true, but I'm *not without* Him. I'm *with* Him.

Paul helped tremendously with my attitude regarding talent when he said, "Try to have a sane estimate of your capabilities" (Rom. 12:3 Phillips' translation).

There it is, two thousand years old and right on target. A *sane estimate!* Very few women have a sane estimate of their talents or life in general. That same verse in the Amplified Bible reads, each one rating "his abilities with sober judgment," never underestimating or *over*-estimating.

The opposite of being humble is being conceited! I know several musicians who are this way and they

29

are extremely temperamental because of it. But, their conceit is an *obvious* kind. I'd like to write about the subtle kind of conceit that inhabits some women (and men) today. They are the women who are always dominating their husband, children, and the whole scene.

A group of us had dinner once with one such woman. She told us what restaurant we'd attend, where to park, and where to wait before we were seated. Her husband stood quietly by, minding his p's and q's and trying not to get in the way. She ordered the food for each of us and after the meal told us when we could leave. She was in her eighties and did all of this with a gracious charm, but that did not disguise the fact that she felt she knew everything there was to know *about* everything. She turned off everyone else's ideas, thoughts, and opinions. She simply had to have the final say. She had so exaggerated her talents and abilities that her conceit had developed into domineering and the absence of humility made her extremely unattractive.

What a waste, I thought. She was intelligent and had had some eighty years of experience she could have shared with us; but she was so busy calling all the shots and making people jump on command that we never really got to know her.

What we need is the lovely balance of Paul's words to form our "estimate of our capabilities." We need to be sane and honest in seeking how to handle our talents.

As I was writing this chapter I was at Hume Lake Christian Camp Grounds in the beautiful mountains above Fresno, California. One afternoon I spoke at a tea for the Hume Lake Women's Auxiliary. I departed from my usual speaking arrangements and asked them if I could share a part of a new book I was writing (this one). I shared my thoughts on humility and invited them to give their ideas.

Afterwards a gifted friend, Bobby Romis, said she'd like to share one thought.

Bobby opened the Old Testament to the familiar passage in Proverbs 31 on "The virtuous woman." When she got to the eighteenth verse she said, "While you were talking about humility and talent I remembered this verse, 'She perceiveth that her merchandise is good: her candle goeth not out by night. She layeth her hands to the spindle, and her hands hold the distaff.'" Then Bobby looked up from her reading and said, "What a woman! She saw her merchandise and knew — no apologies and no bragging — that it was good." The balance of a *sane estimate* is obviously here.

Then Bobby continued, "In other words, she would be the gal who would accept the chairmanship of the Hume Lake Country Fair. She would know how to do it and she would set up committees involving the best women she could find. She would work far into the night to make the Country Fair a success ['. . . her candle goeth not out by night . . .'] and when the fair was over she'd know her 'merchandise was good' and she'd go home and spin wool!

"Look at her. She goes home from being a brainy, hard-working chairman of the fair to spinning wool. She is not insulted at the change in status, no 'poor

31

me' spirit; and because spinning wool takes no mind-bending efforts, she probably takes that time to pray for her husband, children, and business interests. What a woman! She knows her talents are good, stays up to carry them out and is beautifully able to be home spinning wool the following day."

Bobby finished by saying, "I feel God has set up a pattern for us in these two verses: honestly knowing our outside-of-the-home talents; working hard and bringing them into completion; and then, with no problem of adjusting, having a routine day in the home. We need a time to sit, or to be quiet and, yes, even a time to sew, iron, do dishes, using that time to renew our strength and to pray for the dear members of our family."

As Bobby finished her thoughts on this pattern of balance, I thought of the endless number of times I've given concerts, spoken to several hundred women, or counseled with a woman or teenager, and then have come home to the quiet of my sewing room, turned on the iron, and prayed over the clothes as I've ironed. (My favorite humorous writer, Erma Bombeck, says she gets her best ideas for her writings over the ironing board.) When I iron the collar of Dick's shirt I always pray for those neck muscles tired from strain. The sleeves that hold his writing arm get more prayer, and the front panel that covers his heart gets love and prayers. I know the exact place on the back of the shirt that hides a tense vertebra, so I pray especially hard for that spot. Next comes a shirt for Rick and then a dress for Laurie, and they all get thoroughly prayed over. Who's to say the concert takes more talent than the ironing? Not me!

This whole chapter on talent can be summed up in one exciting verse: "God has given each of you some special abilities; be sure to use them to help each other, passing on to others God's many kinds of blessing" (1 Peter 4:10, *Living Bible*).

If we say we have no special abilities, we are calling God a liar. If our motives in being *used* are not to help each other, then we will *not* be "fit vessels" for God to use. If we think talent is only singing or playing piano, we rob others of "God's many kinds of blessings."

Our living in this twentieth-century world does not have to be a boring, worthless, "nothing" type of existence, but the door to real, creative living will remain closed unless the hinges are oiled with a "sane estimate of our capabilities."

Start right now by quitting the tired old routine of "poor me, I have no talents" and begin to take a good look at yourself and your special abilities.

While it might not take too much convincing to tell you your singing talents are not great, you may just find yourself in your kitchen staring down into your gravy skillet. Do you know what talent lumpless gravy requires?

Remember the lady in Okinawa? She asked the Lord to reach down and touch her vision so she could see clearly her talents. She didn't go right out and buy herself a piano so she could begin to play and sing. She simply went home, sensing with new joy her *own* worth and value and knowing her *own* talents.

33

She was a beautiful woman before the service that day, but she carried herself taller and was positively radiant *after* the meeting.

You can have the same joy and radiance, the same feeling of self-worth she got if you'll just let God open your eyes to *your own* special abilities.

The Gentleness and
Mercy Account

The Gentleness and Mercy Account

I might never have found the "Gentleness and Mercy Account" had it not been for a mother, two little boys, and the Alpha Beta Market on the corner . . . but I'm ahead of my story. Let me start by saying that, since I really want to be God's woman, I search His Word daily to find patterns, clues, and His directions for my life. (I followed my own pattern, clues, and directions for some years and never, *never* do I want to go back to that catastrophic way of living!) Every once in awhile I come across a verse that makes absolutely no sense at all to my twentieth-century mind and life. I'll never forget one such verse. There I was quietly minding my own devotions one morning, reading along in Paul's letter to the Philippians when I came to the words, "Let your moderation be known unto all men" (Phil. 4:5).

My eyes read on but my mind stayed behind and began to boggle a bit. So, I re-read it, "Let your moderation be known unto all men." What in the world, what in *my* world did that mean? In the first place, "moderation" simply does not describe me. I'm rarely moderate about anything. If the chicken is absolutely delicious it is *absolutely* delicious, not merely well done. If my hair is a mess, take it from me, it's a mess and *not* somewhere in between. Add to this the fact that part of me is Hungarian and the other part Irish and being outspoken is a normal trait like having one head, one body, two arms, and two legs! My first thought on that verse was, "Well, I'm sure glad Paul wasn't talking to me because I'll never be a moderate, middle-of-the-road person."

As I thought that, I had this mental picture: a Christian living his whole life in moderation, walking the middle of the road, having no outspoken opinions, never making other people happy, sad, angry or anything. It was not possible for me to see myself as this type of person. I'm simply too noisy, too outspoken, too alive to be boxed-in. I dismissed the verse.

However, in the days that followed, the verse would not lie down and be quiet. It kept popping back into my mind, particularly when I felt the need to yell an opinion at Rick or Laurie or voice a strong thought to Dick.

Later that week, since some of my dearest friends are ministers, I thought I'd phone one of them and ask how that verse could be applied to me. But it never seemed to be the right time, and more often than not I'd pass the phone and go put the wash into the dryer. One morning I got to thinking about "direct dialing" and decided to go straight to the top and ask the Lord. The instructions I got sounded like I should read some other translations, so that's where I began.

After much searching I was *convinced* Paul wasn't talking to me. I kept finding words like "forbearance" and "considerateness," and since these are not my strong points, I was about to give up when I looked at one final translation. It was so on target I think I know exactly how Goliath felt just after David did his thing with his trusty sling!

Phillips' translation read, "Have a reputation for gentleness." A reputation for gentleness? *Who, me?* I thought. *No, that's just not my type of personality.*

In *Spirit-controlled Temperament*, Tim LaHaye discusses the four basic human temperaments: the sanguine, the choleric, the melancholy and the phlegmatic.

As you read his book you can identify yourself with one or two of the traits. You may even find that he has accurately pegged your husband's personality, too! I found myself in the middle of the outgoing, talkative sanguine temperament with some of the drive and ambitions of the choleric. Since I identified more with the sanguine, I was very interested in reading everything he had to say about them.

Tim's next book, *Transformed Temperaments,* dealt with St. Paul, the choleric; Moses, the melancholy; Abraham, the phlegmatic, and the sanguine of all sanguines, St. Peter.

Peter had all the traits typical to the sanguine personality — talkative, bold, friendly, and outgoing. He was loved yet seemed always to march in where angels feared to tread. Tim LaHaye describes him as having a tendency toward being rough, impatient, and much like the proverbial "bull in the china shop." So, the command to gentleness gave Peter and all sanguines a real challenge! The only hope for us loud, talkative big-mouths is to be transformed by the Holy Spirit.

Somehow I'd forgotten that lovely redeeming fact. I forgot what a beautiful work the Holy Spirit could do, given any kind of chance. I only knew I was in trouble. *I'm not gentle, I don't see the importance of being gentle, and it's too late in life to get a reputation for it,* I thought. I tried to dismiss the verse, but during the day it clung to my consciousness and it must have wandered in and out of my subconscious thoughts at night because I'd wake in the morning with the verse still in my mind.

I must have mulled and stewed over that verse for weeks when something that sounded remarkably like what my mother would have said rang loud and clear, "When you've tried everything else, you *could* ask the Lord about it, you know!"

So, one morning while I was stewing over this verse, and a cup of coffee, I prayed, "Dear Lord, You *know* (because You made me) gentleness is not exactly my life style. Actually, if I were really honest with You, Lord, I'd have to say I haven't really cared about even wanting gentleness in my life. I figure it's a lost cause — why work for it when it's such a tremendous impossibility? It takes too much time and thought to be gentle, and frankly, I'm too tired to put forth the effort.

"But, Lord, You have gone to great lengths to capture my attention on this subject, and I can no longer ignore the fact that You are eager to teach me this rare and difficult art. Dear Lord, You *do* have Your work cut out for You. I'm not coming into this learning program with very much confidence! You've done some great miracles in my life, but I don't see how I'll *ever* learn. Will You be *most* specific and, remembering my frail mind, give me some down-to-earth, practical illustration?"

When He answered, "Yes," I left it with Him.

The next day I went grocery shopping to get out of the house, and I forgot about gentleness. I applied myself to the task of figuring out how to fill the "bottomless pits" I live with.

The market is about five blocks away from our house. There is nothing particularly religious about its building, parking lot, products, checkers, or box boys, except that one box boy is our son, and come to think of it, there are a whole lot of qualities about him that are remarkably Christ-like. But, for all practical purposes, that market and it's people are just fine for selling groceries but not for teaching theology.

It was late Saturday afternoon by the time I arrived. There couldn't be a worse time to shop, and I hadn't been able to con anyone into coming with me to push my basket or give me moral support as I spent all that money. So, there I was, a bit miserable, pushing my cart, and trying to get the whole thing settled in the shortest amount of time possible.

The problem of racing the clock was aggravated by a roadblock in the first aisle. I couldn't get around a certain shopper no matter *how* I maneuvered. She was a young, beautiful blonde with two cute little boys. One must have been all of five and the other not quite two. From the top of her super-sized pink rollers down to her sandals, the mother was near the edge of hysteria.

I put it all together like this: She had been thinking earlier that afternoon that she'd wash her hair that

41

night, clean up the house later, and do her grocery shopping on Sunday when her husband called and said, "The boss and his wife are coming for dinner tonight."

At least that's what I suspected had happened because she was about as calm as a volcano on the verge of erupting. The boys were "helping" her by handing her this can or that package, and she was trying not to scream as she put each item back on some shelf. (I thought of my son who would be stocking shelves later and would wonder how that sack of sugar got in with the dill pickles.) The boys climbed in and out of the basket and once the little one got into mine. I handed him back and said, "I believe this belongs to you?" She just took him and rolled her eyes toward the ceiling in a most helpless way.

By now we had worked our way through half the store and I continued frantically to try to get past her. No way! Then, when we headed for the wide meat aisle, hope soared within me. I thought, *Aha! I'll cut her off at the pass!* So, I maneuvered, raced, picked up less meat than I intended, and barreled through shoppers with my head lowered for action and my cart sailing along. I made it into the checkout stand and was in the middle of congratulating myself when I looked *ahead* of me and saw the mother and her small boys. By now there was a line behind me so there was no place to go. I mumbled something to myself about "why should I fight it?" when someone tapped me quite sharply on the right shoulder and said, "*Pay attention.*" Since visibly no one was at my right shoulder, I wisely concluded the Lord had spoken.

Once when I was telling this story to several hundred

women, a gal at the close of the meeting came to ask, "Does God *really* tap you on the shoulder and say, 'Pay attention'?"

I answered, "Well, no, actually sometimes He says, "*Sweetie,* pay attention." I wasn't trying to be irreverent or sarcastic. It simply is true that if you and the Lord are on speaking terms and doing as Paul says, "praying without ceasing," there is bound to be a running dialogue between you and the Lord. So you find the grocery store is not too different from whatever spot you choose for your private devotions.

I must confess I really wasn't too sure what I was supposed to pay attention to because at the exact moment the Lord told me to pay attention, the store sort of blew up all around me. I didn't have any trouble in giving the situation my full, undivided attention after that.

It seems the younger boy in that cart ahead of me had run out of wonderful things to do, so he reached up, grabbed the gum and candy rack, and gave it a healthy yank.

As it toppled over it connected its wires with another rack, a large one filled with a jillion candy bars, and the two meshed together and sprayed the front of the store with all kinds of gum, lifesavers, cough drops, and giant Peter Paul Almond Joy bars.

One sixteenth of a second later, the volcano I mentioned earlier erupted into a hot, molten mass of hysterical screaming. All of which was directed, of course, at her two little boys. Everyone was immediately called on duty for a "red alert." Box boys came running from every direction in the store. Personnel who

43

had unwisely chosen to eat their supper in the back room came, and no one was spared the duty of picking up the mess.

Manager, assistants, meat men, clerks and box boys flew into a flurry of action. Kids stuffing all kinds of candy into their pockets were stopped by customers as they raced for the outer doors. Ladies were rolling over fallen Rolaids. Men were softly crushing candy bars to death under their shoes and my feet were absolutely hidden in a sea of lifesavers and Dentyne gum!

By now the volcano was pouring a screaming hot torrent of big words, dirty words, and threatening words into the four little ears below her. She didn't think she was getting through to them so she reached down, grabbed one boy by his sweater collar, the other by one shoulder, swooped them up to eye level, and then really let them have it!

She shook those boys until I was sure blood would come gushing out of any convenient opening, and she let them and everyone else in the store know that they were to *shut up and not move!* After one more violent shake for emphasis, she slammed them down on the floor.

They froze in ramrod positions. I think they even stopped breathing.

Bedlam was still taking place, so she started helping the pick-up crew. I was about to come out of shock and begin to help, too, when the younger boy *moved.*

I was fascinated. He was deliberately disobeying his mother, and I wondered what could motivate such a dangerous action.

To avoid his mother's eyes, he moved like a cautious

snake in slow motion toward his mother's large straw purse and, with deliberate, smooth movements, reached into its depths and inched out a small, faded blue blanket. All the time he was pulling it out of the purse, he never took his eyes from his mother.

Finally he had the blanket tucked under his chin and when he was sure it was there, his tense little shoulders relaxed, he breathed quite a loud sigh and color returned to his face. Tranquillity, as I have rarely seen it, erased the fear from his eyes, and as he began to sway from side to side he ever so gently hummed a little tune. I was completely captivated by this peaceful scene.

The Lord interrupted my thoughts and said, "Here is the down-to-earth lesson I want you to learn. When the little boy's whole world quite literally crashed down around him, *everything* was wrong, and his very life seemed threatened, he did not reach for his nervous, tense, screaming mother, but for his only help — his 'gentler' — his faded, blue blanket, and he was gentled by its presence."

I stood there thinking: his faded patch of blue blanket had probably never given him a moment of pain — never given his teeth a rattling, never given his ears a screaming or threatening lecture; in fact, the only time there was any trouble was when he had temporarily lost it to the washing machine and didn't find it until it came out of the drier. But there in the store, the blanket had been sought, found, used, and the pieces of his whole little world clicked silently back into place. I'm quite sure the checkout girl or a box boy named Jim never knew, as I came through the line, that I was pledging my life to God in a new dimension. I promised the Lord I'd learn all I could about being gentle. I'd let the Holy Spirit take this "sanguine" to school to learn gentleness. I decided that while I had thought gentleness was beyond me, I'd now do everything, with God's help, to be my family's "gentler." I didn't want to leave that work to some synthetic blue blanket, and I thanked God for the gift of gentleness that I knew He was about to give me.

I left that store with a willingness to *earn* a reputation for gentleness. It was an opportunity to grow and I was fascinated by the change of attitude I'd experienced in just a little over an hour.

First, I tried thinking of gentle women I know. I came up with two or three. One was my secretary, Sheila, but holding her up as an example didn't do too much for me because just by her very nature and personality she is gentle and quiet. She never even raises her voice. (I'm convinced she controls her two little children by hidden remote control buttons. It's fantastic!) So, I scrapped that idea.

Finally, after I'd tried to no avail, to manufacture some methods of achieving gentleness, I did what I should have done in the first place. I went back to the Lord. Fortunately, He had waited for me to catch up with Him.

He pointed out that for me gentleness would have to begin in front of my washer. The first person, after me, it would affect was Laurie. He also suggested that when Laurie puts blue jeans with Dick's white shirts, add nylon slips and washes the whole mess on the hot water cycle, I *then* have the opportunity to practice kindness and gentleness.

The whole New Testament is filled with directions for being kind to each other (1 Thess. 2:7, 2 Tim. 2:24, Jas. 3:17, to name a few). Does this mean only to strangers or casual acquaintances? Not exactly. We can start by being kind to our *own* family. Yet, how can I be kind and gentle to a daughter who insists on ruining my wash loads? (Two years ago she went through a "break" cycle and destroyed every glass we had in the whole house!)

I'm quite sure the beginning of gentleness with our own children begins with remembering some of the dumb things we did as youngsters.

My mother's blue cotton dress was a starter. I was fascinated by how quickly bleach put white spots on the navy blue dress. Or, there's the day I was sick with the flu and bored, so I took a razor blade and ripped open all the seams and cording on my grandmother's couch. I was seven years old at the time, but my grandmother, to this day, never misses an opportunity to shake her head and point her finger at me. My list could go on.

I found I could become gentle with Laurie and that stupid wash load if I remembered that for most of my childhood crimes I *was* punished, but it was rarely done out of raw anger. When my mother spanked me, it was by no means a heavy, uncontrollable swing in the dark; it was explained calmly and yes, even gently and then *firmly* applied to my "seat of knowledge." Even in her spank there was a controlled gentleness.

47

Just yesterday I had to go through the this-is-how-we-do-the-wash-honey routine for what seemed to me the eleven millionth time, and would you believe I was kind and gentle? It was accomplished not only by remembering my pledge of gentleness and my childish mistakes, but by recalling the beatitude that says, "Happy are the merciful, for they will have mercy shown to them" (Matt. 5:7, Phillips' translation).

I find I have a whole closet full of gentleness, mercy, and kindness when I take time to remember some of the moments when mercy was shown to me!

Colleen Evans says, "All of us, until we go to be with Christ, will have 'blackouts' in our lives in one area or another." I must remember the times of mercy when I *did not* deserve them — when the blackout was really bad, yet someone was tender toward me. The mistakes, indiscretions, or even plain thoughtless acts of others have been at some time or another my very mistake, my indiscretion, and my thoughtlessness — how dare I forget? I must make allowances for others as I have been given consideration in the past; I must temper my reaction with gentleness, remembering someone's gentleness with me.

There is great merit in the Oriental custom of "saving face." Far too often we are so quick to call a spade a spade, set something immediately right, or instantly correct a situation that we push a person into a corner with absolutely no way to save face. We wonder then why they are so defensive. All we've left the individual is defeat, and he has to come out swinging, ready for a fight.

48

The beatitude about being merciful is a beautiful promise, but it is not without its conditions. *If* I am merciful, I will have mercy shown to me.

The day I began to learn gentleness, I realized how important it was to help Laurie save face. So I took some of the heat out of the conversation by saying, "This is probably *my* fault because I've failed in really teaching and training you to do the laundry. Maybe I wasn't clear enough in my wishes as to when and how to launder. So for that I take the responsibility and the blame."

At this point, instead of her usual lip, Laurie did not become hostile or defensive — she just looked meekly at the washer. I then explained how terribly frustrated I was becoming over these ridiculous wash loads she was running. I don't think it stunts our children's growth to learn that their mother and father have a few hang-ups of their own. How else are our children going to know we are real people with real problems?

What actually was said was not nearly as important as the fact that I was able, in great gentleness and mercy, to discuss a very annoying problem. I'll go through the instructions again when I have to, and I am rather sure that before she gets married and settles down to her own laundry, I'm going to go through it at least a hundred more times. I don't regard this as a chore or duty, nor will you ever catch me saying, "How many *more* times am I going to have to tell Laurie about the wash?" I'm simply going to count this as another opportunity to train her in the art of laundering.

49

Whoops, I think God is about to teach me some more about wisdom, burdens, and gentleness. I found Laurie's jeans have been added to my all-white Clorox wash.

Not long after I decided to spend some funds from the Gentleness Account, I wondered how the Lord would let me show gentleness to our son Rick. Our society would have us believe that after a boy reaches the mature age of four years you don't kiss, hug, or touch him. You make him a "man" by being hard as nails and steeling yourself to show no emotion. You let him know it's not "manly" to cry over a good book or play, and should he be touched by such a book or play and cry, you tell him he's overly sentimental and imply he is not much of a man.

We now have a whole generation of young people, the so-called "hippies," who spend a great deal of time touching and sharing food and bed and laughter and tears. I think I can understand the reaction that has driven them to express so vividly the gamut of emotions and reach out to one another to be touched.

In our home we have made quiet but continued efforts not only to touch and kiss our children, but to tell them (out loud, not just by slipping them some extra money) that they are loved. Also, we have endeavored to give our children *time*. We felt that our son needed to learn about a gentle woman and a gentle man from his parents if he was to know gentleness himself and if he were to be a gentle husband-father-adult.

The opportunity presented itself clearly one after-

50

noon when Rick came home from school, obviously distressed. Since I have become aware of the art of gentleness, I've learned to slow down my typical motherly pounce, so I waited a bit and then quietly probed, "Something wrong?"

The answer, "Oh, Mom," just heaved out and he continued, "I've just seen an awful thing. The guy who sits next to me in drama class had taken acid [LSD] between periods and when we were twenty minutes into class this guy went absolutely berserk. His face, his eyes, everything was so horrible."

He went on for a few minutes describing what had happened next and how it took four boys to get him out to a friend's van.

Rick was emotionally spent, having witnessed so close at hand someone completely out of his head because of a bad drug trip. It was the moment for gentleness, so, without a word I crossed the kitchen floor to where Rick stood, put my arms around his six feet of manhood and held him close for many minutes.

I found out in those moments that I wanted to be the "gentler" not only in disciplining and training my children but in sensing their special needs mentally and spiritually. Those moments in the kitchen soothed and healed Rick's very bruised mind.

After a bit he straightened up and looked down at me saying, "Mom, when I was a baby I probably needed to be held — but *never* more than just now." I left the kitchen with my eyes stinging with tears. I had almost *not* gone to him because of all that stupid brainwashing about letting a grown boy heal his own wounds. I also walked away from the experience wondering *who* would gentle him if his mother or father did not? What teacher, friend, or neighbor would gentle his grieved mind? What type of blue blanket would he turn to if he failed to find it at home? Where would he have turned had I not responded to God's leading? The responsibility to be a gentle woman was and is awesome!

Those experiences with our children were lovely training sessions in how the richest lady in town should spend some of her great wealth. They were also just the preliminary training grounds for learning about gentleness as a wife.

I've always been a firm believer in greeting my husband cheerfully and loudly as he gets home from work, dropping everything to go meet him! I take his coat and that morning cereal bowl out of his hand (he eats breakfast while being bored in our slow, rush hour, morning freeway traffic). Giving him a big kiss and equally big hello are just part of every evening ritual with us.

Usually I'm my noisy, bouncy self and I streak out to the garage, bang the car door open and fairly yell, "Hello, sweetie!" It occurred to me there were a remarkable number of times when Dick seemed less than enthusiastic at my greetings, and sometimes he just straightened up, put his hand to his head and quietly muttered something about, "Please, Joyce, later."

I felt perhaps this was one area where I could be gentle, I decided to try it. The next night I didn't hear his car drive into the garage. He had opened the front door before I came face to face with him. Instead of flying at him with my usual verve, I stood very quietly beside him, took his things and whispered, "Hello, sweetie." He just stood there surveying the new, quiet me, and after a second, took his things out of my hands, put it all on the hall shelf, gently pulled me into his arms and gave me a super-cinemascope-living-color-motion-picture-schmaltzy kiss! After my lungs took up breathing again, my ears heard him say, "I *really* love you."

"Why?" I gasped.

He put both hands on my shoulders and said shaking his head, "Because you're always in there trying!" He was smiling, but we both knew he had been "gentled."

It was very clear in that moment that the world of banking, pressures, and tensions my husband faced could be dropped at the end of the day if I inspired it by building a bridge of quiet gentleness. It also occurred to me, as it had with the children, that if I was not gentle, who would be? Perhaps some day, in some bank, some cute teller would cross the lobby to the management side, stop at Dick's desk and say, "Mr. Landorf, I just want to tell you I think you're really nice." I'm certain even her good looks and short skirt would go unnoticed because of her gentle words. Perhaps, just perhaps, if he had not heard gentleness in my voice at home, it would sound very appealing in hers at the bank.

I have, from that day in the hall to this day, changed my tone of voice in greeting and in conversations with my husband. I'm determined to drop nagging phrases (*"You would,* wouldn't you?"*) or whining sentences (*"You never* listen to me anymore") and in their place insert mercy, tenderness, kindness, and, above all, gentleness.

I'll tell you right now, when Dick presses me into a commitment about *when* I'm going to throw away the moldy leftovers in the fridge, it's not easy to be a lovely pile of soft gentleness! (Sometime I re-read my own books.) Actually, this Gentleness Account has just barely been dipped into. I have a lot of learning and living to do in Christ, but I am really excited about this account and all its possibilities!

James knew about this account and quite often he coupled gentleness with wisdom: "But the wisdom that is from above is first pure, then peaceable, *gentle*, and easy to be intreated, full of mercy and good fruits, without partiality, and without hypocrisy" (3:17).

Tucked away in Proverbs is the ancient wisdom, "Gentle words cause life and health; griping brings discouragement" (Prov. 15:4, *Living Bible*). Gentleness gives my family "life and health" in this time of crisis living and strained mental and physical health. I'd be a fool to ignore the treasures contained in gentleness.

When I was about seven, the circus came to town. I begged my mother to let me go with some friends to watch the unloading of animals in the railroad freight yards. She reluctantly let me go with the stern warning to "be back in two hours."

Of course, it was all so interesting we lost any concept of time and only as we were running home did we realize it was almost dark and we'd been gone many hours.

When I came breathlessly through the front door I

found my mother on the couch, eyes red from crying. All she said was, "Oh, Joyce!" I knew that second that she had been sure I was hurt, lost, kidnapped, or all three.

I'll never forget what happened. Even though she was obviously happy to see me, she still firmly spanked me to impress me with the fact that I'd disobeyed her. I was duly impressed. But what I remember most was that after the spanking, when I was sobbing alone in my room, she came in, took me in her arms, settled me down on her lap, and explained once more why it was wrong to break rules. Then she carefully comforted and gentled me by assuring me of her love. I never loved her more.

In Isaiah, God tells His people, "I will comfort you there as a little one is comforted by its mother" (Isa. 66:13, *Living Bible*).

I'm too grown up now to climb on my mother's lap to be comforted and gentled, yet this beautiful passage in Isaiah is a treasure house of gentleness that God has given to me. More than once, as a wife and mother, I've needed to be gentled and God has done it not only through my family but directly, too.

Jesus Himself, our great pace-setter for right now, said, "Wear my yoke — for it fits perfectly — and let me teach you; for I am gentle and humble, and you shall find rest for your souls; for I give you only light burdens" (Matt. 11:29, 30, *Living Bible*).

The Opportunity Account

The Opportunity Account

Usually when people are on the lowest rung of the economic ladder, the only thing they care about is to be raised as many rungs as possible in the shortest amount of time.

Just today I opened a national magazine and read *another* article on "Welfare and How I Get Along." This morning's newspaper had a quaint little story on the front page about an executive who could hardly "get by" on the $30,000 he was making a year. In the same paper was an article about a poor woman who had inherited $200,000 and spent it all the same year. Columns on money, money management, investments, etc. are abundant. With all of this storehouse of information available to us, you'd think we'd all be wealthy.

Everywhere I turn someone is talking about money or the lack of it. Being married to a banker doesn't help much either. What comes through loud and clear is the idea, "For goodness' sake, don't be poor. It's the most undesirable situation in the world. Avoid poverty like the plague!"

I was born in 1932, and since that year followed

1929, '30 and '31 we all know what kind of baby I was. My mother never got around to calling those years "depression years"; they were always "opportunity years."

She saw the fact that dad was making $3.00 a week in his little church, not as the meager sum it was, but as some giant opportunity to trust God. If she longed for wealth, she never nagged or complained to dad or others about it. She held up our poverty before the Lord, fully expecting Him to take care of it. He never failed her.

She never whined or pined for the clothes and furniture she didn't have. She took what she had and expected the Lord to make her extremely creative. He did, many times beyond her expectations — or ours.

Whoever said, "Necessity is the mother of invention," never knew my mother, but if he had, he would have dedicated that saying to her.

The hardship of being poor in the early thirties forced to the surface one rich dividend after another.

I didn't know we were poor until I was graduating from high school and then I found out only by accident. By that time my father was dean of men at a small Bible college in California. His salary was: Board — like all institutional food, room — a few tiny rooms packed into the end of the boys' dorm, and salary — $150 per month. I had no idea we had so little.

My mother would bring that horrible dining hall food into our rooms, whisper lovingly to it, add a bit of this or that, and it actually tasted very good! Necessity and poverty made her an excellent cook. She'd

60

collect broken, unused furniture no one else wanted, fix, paint, antique, and lovingly coax it into delightful tables, chairs and couches. She found that an old beat-up cotton rug purchased at the Goodwill store could be cut down, washed, and dyed a bright color. We had fancy "area rugs" long before some whiz-bang interior decorator ever invented them.

I remember her reputation on that campus. Gals were always dropping in on Mrs. Miller to see "what she's done now."

I never dreamed that taking one's poverty in stride, using it to really trust the Lord, and expecting Him to help you be extremely creative was not the normal, everyday thing all Christians did. And I never suspected I was living with a woman who was extraordinarily rich.

James has a verse which describes her very well: "God has chosen poor people to be rich in faith" (2:5, *Living Bible*). I didn't recognize her great storehouse of wealth until three weeks before my high school graduation.

I was to be graduated from Pasadena City College which at that time was a four-year institution, the last two years of high school and the first two years of college. Each year the two graduating classes had one graduation in the giant Rose Bowl. Twelfth graders (that was me) graduated in white formals. The fourteenth graders were dressed in traditional cap and gown.

Mother showed no sign of hysteria when I said I needed a long, white formal, even though she had no idea where I'd get one. She just took me shopping the next day in all the fancy stores, and I tried on one lovely dress after another. We didn't buy any because, as she told the clerks, "We're just looking and getting a feel for what we want."

What really unhinged my jaw and produced a lot of oohing and ahhing from my mother was a beautiful, full-skirted organdy dress, with a hand-tucked bodice embroidered with tiny seed pearls, and a skirt with tucks all the way to the floor. Mother, after she stopped oohing and ahhing, said quite casually as she turned the price tag over, "Oh, that's what daddy makes in a month."

I was stunned. "A *month?*" It was my first clue that we were poor. We were next to welfare and I'd never known it!

At school all the next day, I thought about my poverty-stricken state and that unobtainable white dress. I could easily visualize graduation night with all the girls in beautiful white gowns, and me, in the middle of them, resplendent in my sweatshirt and blue jeans. I mulled over the problem all the way home that day and was nowhere near ready for the scene that met me in our living room.

My mother was sewing, and flowing from her beat-up sewing machine was a long, white, full organdy skirt, tucked every six inches to the bottom. The bodice was lying on the dining room table all put together, and at one glance I could tell where I'd sew two bottles of tiny seed pearls. I was so carried away with the dress, Mother's happy chatter, and visions of graduation night, I forgot to ask where the material came from.

I slipped off my school clothes and was in the middle of my fitting session when I noticed the marvelous quality of the organdy and finally had the presence of mind to ask, "By the way, where did you get this beautiful stuff?"

Mother took the pins out of her mouth, smiled, shrugged her shoulders, and said, "Oh, it's just some I had here." She went back to her pinning.

I thought, *Some she had here?* and then the horrible truth dawned.

"Mother," I yelled, "this organdy was the beautiful crisscrossed curtains we *used* to have in the dining room!"

"Mmmm, right." She went right on and never missed a pin.

Now I *really* knew the facts:

1. We were poor.
2. It didn't matter.
3. I had an extraordinary mother!

Without even wincing, my mother had cut up her treasured organdy curtains. No regrets, no martyr complex, no "poor me," no lecture on how long she had saved to buy them on sale; just this — "I need a long white dress for Joyce. Ah, yes, the organdy curtains. They'll do nicely." Snip, snip.

The dress still hangs in my closet and it is the best reminder of what treasures poverty *can* bring. It also makes me smile when I remember the seating arrangement of graduation night. I sat between two of the wealthiest girls in Pasadena's social register. They spent the whole time telling me how fantastic my dress was. "A little something my mother whipped up," I kept saying.

We are continually being told today how awful it is not to have everything. Besides, the newspaper and magazine articles I mentioned, we have television hammering home its golden message of BUY, BUY, BUY!

Each commercial tells us that if we have this product we will be either

1. happy
2. satisfied
3. beautiful
4. smart

or all four. This kind of advertising, over a long period of time, leads us to believe that we must *have* everything offered for sale or our lives will be dull and incomplete. So we have a mad, insane wish to buy and accumulate things. That is the best and surest way to deprive God of the opportunity to be trusted, to perform miracles, and to provide in powerful, exciting ways beyond our expectation.

We put fantastic limits on God and I feel that's one of our biggest mistakes. We miss so much. You see, what made my childhood a choice adventure was the fact that my parents never really knew how God was going to act, only that He *would*.

One time when my dad was still making only $3.00 a week, my parents were down to their last fifty cents.

My folks had discussed the food they needed and just how they'd spend that fifty cents. Mother got carried away and imagined how good bacon sounded and tomato juice and pineapple and so on. Before too long she had an unrealistic list of twenty-one items.

64

Dad advised her that even in the depression, fifty cents wasn't going to go that far.

Later, as dad drove to the store to buy just some essentials, one tire decided not to cooperate, breathed out its final breath, and went flat. The nice man at the service station said he could install a new boot so the tire would last a few more months and that it would only cost — you guessed it — fifty cents.

Dad recalled those days for me vividly just the other night. He told me of driving slowly home and breaking the news to mother. He said since their shopping plans had been changed, they decided to have a prayer meeting for two — not a sad prayer meeting but a joyous one. It was a prayer meeting of two people in love with the Lord and each other. They thanked the Lord that they *did* have, if nothing else, the precious gift of eternal life.

The next thing they did was sing the Doxology together. "Praise God from whom all blessings flow." Almost forty years later my father's eyes glistened with tears as he remembered how happily they sang that day.

Their singing in those circumstances was wonderfully Christ-like; maybe that's why God was so spectacular in the following moments.

After the singing mother went into the kitchen and there on the table were two large bags of groceries. She called dad and together they began unloading the cans and boxes of food. Their amazement blossomed into reverent awe as they realized that not only did they have essential food items mysteriously deposited on their kitchen table but every item my mother had so whimsically wanted as well.

The bacon, tomato juice, pineapple — they were all there. There were more than twenty-one items. They had no idea who was responsible for their bountiful supply except that God had heard their prayers. Then they really sang out the Doxology!

Over a year later a man in dad's church said, "By the way, a long time ago I got sick on my job and I asked if I could go home. The boss let me, but by the time I reached home I was fine and decided to return to work. However, my wife was standing in the driveway and said, 'I know *why* you're home. Rev. Miller needs some groceries so let's go to the store.'

"So, we went to the store and my wife went down one aisle and I took the other until we had all the items. We *knew* which ones to pick. Then, when we got to your back door we could hear you praying and singing. We didn't want to bother you, so we just set the groceries on the table and left. You did get them, didn't you?"

All through their lives my parents watched God work His miracles.

In one of my mother's many notebooks I found something that really summed up her attitude toward financial matters.

"In life you strive and reach out for gold.
In heaven you walk on it!"

In poverty she had been truly blessed and as I grew up she passed those blessings on to me.

We had no money for concerts, going abroad for

66

study, or learning the fine arts, but she never let that hinder my cultural education.

When we lived in Michigan we took long streetcar rides across Detroit and spent many hours looking, listening, and learning in the Detroit Institute of Arts Museum. One part of the museum I'll *never* forget was the Egyptian section. Mother never got to travel to the Holy Lands even though she reminded the Lord of it many times. The next best thing was taking me to the Egyptian section and seeing mummies and biblical artifacts. To this day I never see anything about the Holy Land without remembering those happy times of learning.

Poverty taught her to develop the art of observing. Traveling across Detroit on a streetcar with her was quite an adventure because she'd force me to see all there was to see, to look and watch, to be aware of everything.

Now that I have my own children, I've spent many times riding San Francisco cable cars with them, teaching and training them to see all there is. I received the ability to observe and perceive because we were too poor to own a car. I have a rich inheritance because of our poverty.

The stories of how God met my parent's needs were told to me and are repeated now to my children. How my parents trusted the Lord, and He provided not only food, clothing, and money, but profound lessons in living!

Aside from reliving and enjoying these stories of God's provisions in my family's past, I never really opened my own Opportunity Account until it was

67

thrust upon me — inappropriately, I thought at the time.

It was just about seven years ago. My husband, Dick, had been in charge of a large toy store in Pomona when he was offered the opportunity to manage a large department store. He went from managing twenty or thirty employees (at peak Christmas time) to a large store with some sixty to seventy employees. The transition was rough, but we were sure God had opened this door in a fantastic way. We praised Him for this new, challenging job. We were sure that He was in this new move.

Dick really didn't care for the retail business, but his college work was all in business administration, and never at any time did he consider anything but retail (or wholesale) selling as a life's occupation. He had risen to the top in every job he had ever held from the time he was a box boy in his teens through this point in his life.

But less than three months after we "knew" God had given him this advancement, Dick came home from work with the personal articles from his desk in one hand and two weeks' severance pay in the other.

"I was called into the main store and fired this afternoon," he explained in a stunned tone of voice. He took his role of breadwinner with utmost conscientiousness and to be fired was an experience he never thought he'd have.

My surprise gave way to instant tears, not because of the financial problems we would be facing, but because there stood my husband, a *new* man of God who honestly wanted only to do and obey God's will, who had never been fired from any job; in one afternoon his whole world collapsed.

I'll never forget that afternoon or evening. We cried, we prayed, we talked, we rehashed this whole venture. We read the Scriptures and came up with not one single clue as to why this had happened.

Some time during the afternoon I heard Satan's snappy little voice crack, "So, now you are Christians and look what happens! God told you to quit your other job and take this one, didn't He? See how God *loves* you? How He rewards you? How will you live? What will you do? Jobs are scarce. How will you feed your children?"

The afternoon came to an ironic climax. At 6:30 p.m. we had to go to a church dinner for about thirty couples, and I was the main speaker. They had given me the topic, "How God Leads Us in a Christian Marriage."

I had a microscopic amount of willingness to go to that dinner, but a funny thing happened to me as I was about to speak.

The Lord said, "All afternoon you and Dick have listened to each other. Later you listened to Satan, but now, sweetie, you listen to me!"

So, once more I stood before a group of older, wiser adults, opened my mouth, asking the Holy Spirit to speak, and to my incredible amazement He *did*.

I traced the Lord's hand in our marriage up to the present time and then, without sharing that Dick had been fired that day, I told them we were experiencing the greatest challenge and opportunity of our lives. It was, to date, the most contradictory time of our lives,

69

yet *we were going to trust the Lord anyway.* Before I ended I could see the Lord had already touched Dick's heart. His head was up and, while he had not a clue in the world as to what would happen, Dick's shoulders were straight and the peace and confidence that only God can give were in his face and eyes.

During the next months of unemployment I dipped into the opportunity account with a heavy hand. I learned 250 ways to be creative with one pound of hamburger. I began to teach myself how to sew. I made drapes for Rick's room, fancy French valances and curtains for Laurie's room, braided rugs, sewed all Laurie's and my clothes, and managed all that on a $12 treadle sewing machine Dick had bought me at an auction. Since I *never* had the patience to sew even a straight seam before, this was the most fascinating, exciting time of my life.

I did find though, that in the beginning I could only sew for a maximum time of ten minutes. I've increased now, but I do remember praying over that sewing machine, being frustrated by a difficult collar or sleeve, and hearing the Lord say, "Leave this machine and go do the dishes." I did and later, when I returned to sew the collar or sleeve, it just zipped into place without a whimper.

Dick was still without work when someone suggested he take an aptitude test to see what kind of work he'd really be suited to do. So he did, and when the results came back they showed he could do just about anything he wanted. That was *no* help at all. But the Lord used the test to show that in financial matters Dick rated particularly high, and this caused him to recall that in retail management he had liked the financial side best.

He had lunch with a mortgage broker from our church and came home with a job. In a brief span of time he became the vice president of this small but active loan company. Now we knew it was God who had fired Dick. Dick was too conscientious to leave the retail field just because he didn't like it. It took an out-and-out firing to move him. So that was precisely how God acted.

About this time we phased out the Opportunity Account because we were getting financially secure; then the whole bottom dropped out of the mortgage loan business in California. My husband and hundreds of loan men like him were out of work with no place to go. We reopened the Opportunity Account very quickly. This time, however, there were no tears, no panic, and not even a period of Satan-inspired depression. Dick quietly laid out our financial problems on the table and said, "Uh, You see this mess, Lord?" The Lord's peace was so strong we were both almost giddy. That's what James meant when he said, "Consider yourselves happy indeed . . . with trials of every sort" (1:2, Knox's translation).

We had a happy, joyous spirit. It was ridiculous to be at such peace when everything was wrong, yet that's exactly how it was.

Dick said, rather matter-of-factly, "Honey, it's very possible we will lose this house, our cars and most of our furniture, so I want you to plan accordingly."

Being strictly female I could lose the cars without too big an adjustment and maybe the house, but the

71

furniture? I didn't know — that was a different story. I didn't feel too "happy" all of a sudden. (I find my spiritual level has a tendency to go up and down like a yo-yo.)

However, it was at this point that the Opportunity Account reminded me of its availability, and while I wasn't about to call a joyous singing prayer meeting as my parents had, I did go to the Lord with these words, "Father, if we lose the house and cars, that's really all right, but dear Lord, about the *furniture*. . . . You know how I shopped, fixed, mended, upholstered, painted, or antiqued nearly every piece? I'm terribly fond of those chests, tables, and chairs. Help!"

"If you lose every stick of furniture in the whole house, Joyce, what have you lost . . . really? You and Dick are still My children." The Lord's unruffled answer stung its way home to me. I've never been too keen on having my security ruined or even threatened, and somehow my furniture had become my blue blanket — without my realizing it. The beatitude says, "Happy are those who claim nothing, for the whole earth will belong to them" (Matt. 5:5, Phillips' translation). The beauty of those words broke over me. It was silly to be so concerned about tables and chairs even if I *did* practically make them.

So, I went to Dick and said, "If we lose everything, what have we really lost? Pieces of wood, fabrics, glass, motors, but nothing more. We may have to live in a tent and (perish the thought) camp out for years, but so what? We still have each other, we have Rick and Laurie, and more important than that, we have Christ — *living in us*.

We began to thank God for the lay-off and watched for God's magnificent hand to begin working. Months later when Dick was offered a starting trainee position in a bank, our financial crisis eased and our losses were light. The lesson was marvelous for us because we could have lost everything. Yet we had been able to realize we would have survived, in fact, as James said, we would have been able to *rejoice* in our troubles, because they would have added to our growth.

In the past few years, God has allowed us to accumulate some earthly things and we are learning to enjoy them without their owning us. For instance, in our living room we have white shag carpeting, pale blue chairs, and blue-and-white print couches, all blending into a restful, peaceful room. Besides teaching me how to make something out of nothing, my mother showed me how to take a small treasure and turn it into a large beauty, and the room reflects all of this.

But there is one thing I'd like to make very clear about this room. If I lost the entire room and all its lovely things, pictures, accessories, the piano, and the white carpet, my world would not collapse and neither would I. Truthfully, I'd miss those lovely, rather irreplaceable things, but they are not my whole world. My trust and faith are not in them and they do not own me. I do not really own them either. They are a generous loan to me from the Lord.

I am afraid too many women today put all their hopes and dreams into furniture, houses, and things only to find, if suddenly they lose those possessions, they are stunned with the loss and are unable to function as persons.

We do the same thing sometimes in regard to possessing people. "Oh, I'd die if anything happened to my husband; or, "If I lost my son in war, I don't know how I'd exist," we say. But the truth is, God gives us people and things and they are really on loan to us. I want to enjoy husband, children, house, and furniture and to love them for what they really are — *gifts!* It is possible to spend a whole lifetime possessing people and things and miss the joy of knowing how to *trust* the Lord.

If God has entrusted money or possessions to your care, remember it is what you *do* with your wealth that really counts, and whether or not it runs you or you run it. Use your wealth for His glory. Thank Him constantly and seek His Holy Spirit for direction.

On the other hand, if God has allowed you to live in a measure of poverty — American women know nothing of being poor compared to many women of the world — then use your lack of worldly possessions to make you rich in faith. My mother did, and it not only made her rich in faith, but in a hundred creative ways she never suspected. If you are poor by our American standards but have learned to thank God and have responded to the unique challenge, you can be the richest lady in town.

In one of those endless notebooks, my mother wrote, "If God is going to do something wonderful — He starts with a problem. If God is going to do something spectacular — He starts with an impossibility."

My family is still learning about the dividends of

74

being poor. My sister, Marilyn, almost twenty, was studying in Israel this summer. She had prayed in all her expense and flight money and even secured a $500 loan. When she first told me she had the chance to study in the Holy Land and receive ten units of credit, we were jubilant over the thought of it. But the cost was over $1500, and as far as Marilyn was concerned it could have been 15 million. Yet we trusted that if the Lord wanted her to go, He'd supply the money. I desperately wished I was enormously wealthy and could foot the whole bill. Yet, that would have deprived us of using the Opportunity Account; it would have put God in a remote position and I would have never seen Him in action quite so vividly! Just two days before she was to leave, the Lord told some friends to give her the last of the $1500 she needed. She went off to Israel really praising God!

There was little extra spending money available to her while she was there. She had worked all school year and, with the help of some scholarships, had barely made it through school financially, so extra money was non-existent. Once when her only pair of sandals fell apart she simply prayed over their tattered remains, telling the Lord of her needs and *thanking* Him that her only pair of sandals had fallen apart.

The next day an American woman studying at the same Institute came to Marilyn and said, "Honey, God has laid it on my heart to buy you some sandals." It was as simple as that. All summer long God provided just enough money from different sources and in beautiful ways, even though at one point Marilyn and her roommate, Barbara, had their money stolen.

75

At the end of the summer, Marilyn counted out what money was left. She knew she would need money for food in Rome on the trip home. She had enough for the four days in Rome since her hotel and flight were prepaid, but the day before she was to leave Israel, she found she needed ten pounds for an exit tax.

She did not tell anyone, not even her roommate, that she was short ten pounds, but she breathed to the Lord, "Lord, You know in order for me to leave this country tomorrow You have to pay the ten pounds — I don't have it. I thank You that I *don't* have the ten pounds." And with that she left it in God's lap. She was well into the Opportunity Account.

She finished classes and exams, then checked her mail box to see if she'd received a letter from home, but the box was empty. Still, she told no one of her need.

Later that night she thought she'd check her box one more time and when she peeked down into it she could see some paper all folded up. She said she just smiled when she saw her name scribbled on top because all summer she had been putting little happy faces, notes, poems, etc. in everyone's box and she was just sure someone was sending her a fun note or poem.

She opened the sheet of paper and ten pounds fluttered down to the floor. For a moment she just stood there looking at the money and then slowly she opened up the paper.

It read:

> To Marilyn
> Love, Jesus

To this day she does not know the name of the human heart God used to work this spectacular "impossibility" but Marilyn had a first-hand experience of watching the Opportunity Account in action.

Marilyn is like my mother — poor in the things of this world, but rich in faith. Remember, she would *never* be really rich in faith *without the times of poverty.*

A friend of ours has just opened up this account as I found out by his Christmas letter. We get our share of Christmas letters each year, but this one was extra special. It was a typical long, newsy letter, interesting only to dear friends, but I'd like to share some parts of it here. He wrote:

> This past year has been one of the most discouraging for our family. Two days before last Christmas I was laid off from work and was out of work for almost four months. I just couldn't find work anywhere. We were not prepared financially for this disaster. But with God's help and guidance and assistance from relatives and friends, we have withstood the strain. We give God all the praise, because without our faith in Him, we would have given up and almost lost everything.
>
> We did have to sell our trailer, which upset our kids, but they understood what we were going through.
>
> In April I started work as a salesman. My neighbor was quite instrumental in getting me the job. I never sold anything in my lifetime, so I was scared stiff on my first day. But with God's help I learned very quickly. At the end of each month I would generally end up in the top fifteen salesmen out of

thirty-five men — you must agree, I couldn't have done it without His help.

We had a wonderful Christmas last year despite all our problems. It is a wonderful, warm feeling to know that the Lord is with you — through good and bad times.

We're so grateful for our kids and our family life!"

Then, after a personal rundown on his children, he ended by saying,

I know this is a much more serious letter than usual — but we want others who have faced these problems, or those who might have to face them in the future — to have faith in God. He will give you direction — if you believe in Him.

And of course last, but most important, is my wonderful wife, Connie. Without her strength and love, I would have given up a long time ago. During troubled times — if a family isn't pulling together — complete failure would set in! But God strengthened our love for Him as well as our love for each other. Our love for each other is stronger now than ever before.

In closing, if the Lord can provide a Jewish man (my neighbor) to help a Christian (me) to get a job — then He can perform miracles for you!

As I finished his letter I realized I had read the writings of a wealthy man. He had his perspectives and goals in the right order. He and his wife had learned that the secret of adjusting and accepting problems was to be found in first rejoicing in them. Their growth was obvious.

Not too many months after I'd read his letter I was reading 2 Corinthians 4 from *The Living Bible* and thought once more, very vividly of this friend.

> We are pressed on every side by troubles, but not crushed and broken. We are perplexed because we don't know why things happen as they do, but we don't give up and quit. We are hunted down, but God never abandons us. We get knocked down, but we get up again and keep going. . . . These troubles and sufferings of ours are, after all, quite small and won't last very long. Yet this short time of distress will result in God's *richest* blessing upon us forever and ever. So we do not look at what we can see right now, the troubles all around us, but we look forward to the joys in heaven which we have not yet seen. The troubles will soon be over, but the joys to come will last forever (vv. 8, 9, 17, 18).

The Opportunity Account is one of the biggest available to the Christian.

The Resource Account

The Resource Account

Clare Bauer, a dear friend of mine, bounced into my living room, barely said hello, and fired off at me, "Okay, so you're writing a third book. Is it about your mother?"

My round-about answer was, "Well, no, it isn't, but yes, in a way it is."

"You've got to write about her. *That's* the book I'm waiting for," she said indignantly.

"I am, I am," I countered, "but I'm not writing her whole life's story. I'm just making her a part of the book in various chapters."

Clare didn't look too pleased and I had to smile. There she sat asking me to write about a woman she'd never met and had never laid eyes on. My mother died before Clare had even met me, yet Clare was asking — no, really pleading with me to write of my mother.

"Please write of her. From what you and your sister Marilyn have told me I know others need to hear about this remarkable woman," Clare said, restating her feelings.

My mother was indeed a remarkable woman. She influenced us and hundreds of other people in fantastic ways, even after her death.

My brother Cliff's wife, Bonita, said recently to my sister, "There's one woman I really want to be like. That's your mother."

Marilyn responded, "But you've never met her. She died before you even knew Cliff."

"Yes, I know," Bonita said, "but everyone who ever did know her talks about her, and they never mention what she *looked* like. They simply talk on and on about her relationship with God. She must have been a real woman of God, and I want to be just like her."

Breast cancer took everything from her except the sparkling spirit that fairly danced out of her dark brown eyes. In less than three years after her mastectomy and halfway through her fifty-seventh year, the Lord said, "That is *absolutely all* the pain I will allow her to bear," and He issued the command for Death to bring her to Him.

She went more than willingly, but we let her go with halting reluctance. We dressed her in her favorite flowered voile dress, surrounded her with a huge garden of flowers and packed in dad's church with hundreds of people who listened to her funeral service.

John Gustafson's voice rang out in her favorite songs, "Until Then" and "My Heavenly Father Watches Over Me"; Chuck Leviton read a poem he had composed about her, "Marion Miller, the Quiet Fanatic"; Dr. Ted Cole preached a stirring message about her life ending with "She is *not* dead." Then we all stood and sang "Great Is Thy Faithfulness" and watched as dear and precious people filed past us. We said our goodbys and tearfully watched as the casket lid was closed upon her.

It should have been the end of her, but then we found all her notebooks: big spiral ones, little spiral ones, date books, secretary pads, loose-leaf binders, and even her diary kept before she met my father. They were a treasure house of ideas, theories, and inspiration — the essence of fifty-seven years of being God's woman.

Once, when she was being introduced to speak for a large group of women, the mistress of ceremonies referred to Marion Miller as a "real, live saint of God."

I was sitting next to my mother and I leaned over and penciled in on the top of her notes, "Hey, how about that, you're a real, live *saint* of God!"

Her deep brown eyes really came alive, and she took my pencil and wrote on the margin of my Bible, "Look out when anyone calls you a saint. It's a funny thing about saints — God usually calls them home!"

She would not like me to write of her as some stiff, pious, holy saint for she was nothing like that. She was a real, live woman, with a real, live husband, three children, and two grandchildren. She taught four Bible classes each week. She taught Christian release time with children each week. She worked at everything in dad's church from refinishing all the pews in the main sanctuary to being Sunday school superintendent and DVBS coordinator each summer. She was the spiritual advisor for a Christian sorority, Lambda Theta Chi, and the local PTA. Toward the end of her life she suffered the real, live pain that only cancer is capable of inflicting.

She was *no* saint, but she lived her fantastic life one moment at a time. The only thing different about her was that she managed that life with a running dialogue with her best friend, Jesus. And *that*, my friend, really set her apart!

She was so connected with the Lord that she knew the exact moment to look at a child, teenager, young adult, or senior citizen and say, "By the way, there's someone I'm just dying for you to meet. He's my friend. Let me introduce you to Him." Then calling the person by his name she'd bring him to the Lord.

Just this week as I was reading a great little book, *Witness Is Withness* (Moody Press, 1971) I thought of my mother's unique ability to share the love and joy of Christ with just anyone. The author of that book, David Augsburger, would have loved her because she lived out his subtitle, "More showing than telling."

The last year of her life, in spite of enormous pain, she introduced so many people to the Lord it would have been impossible to keep track of all of them. Her counseling ministry was so heavy that in her last year, in order for me to talk with her, I had to go to her home, pick her up, and take her shopping. Once when I arrived to pick her up she shushed me up and hustled me down the hall into the den. I glimpsed a tense, drawn young woman sitting on the edge of mother's living room couch as I went flying by. Some two hours later, after I'd read a couple of books, Mother came in just radiant.

"We can go now," she said cheerily. I barely heard

her because I was staring at a small, pearl-handled revolver in her hand.

"Oh, that," she said. "Well, the young lady in the living room came early this morning determined to use this on herself if God didn't answer her. We've prayed and talked and God really came through. She left, having met the Savior — and said she didn't need this anymore."

I probably was the only shopper walking around the May Company that day with her mouth hanging open.

Her work with the PTA was equally amazing. I don't know how they did it, but a PTA board made up entirely of Jewish women elected my mother, the Gentile wife of the local Community Church minister, to be their Spiritual-Inspiration Chairman year after year, long after her kids were graduated! It was not without a minor problem in the beginning.

The first Christmas she served on the board, she was instructed to refrain from talking about Christmas. She would be allowed to talk only about Hanukkah. She talked that over with the Lord and came to the board with the observation that Christmas was not just a Gentile holiday but a national one, and that it would be unpatriotic to ignore it; furthermore, she had boned up on Jewish tradition and was fully qualified to speak on both Christmas and Hanukkah, which she did. In fact, her presentation to a packed auditorium was so marvelous, the local rabbi asked to meet her, as he called her the "storehouse of information called Marion Miller, wife of a minister!"

Year after year they called her back to serve. She never compromised her Christian testimony, but at the same time the Lord wisely led her into a ministry of inspiring hundreds of Jewish women about their special Hebrew heritage. Many of them quietly accepted their Messiah.

We got a glimpse into what mother must have meant to these women when just hours after she died the PTA president pressed a large, bulging envelope into my Dad's hands and said, "Reverend Miller, no one asked for this or started it; it was a spontaneous act. When the word came about Marion this morning, PTA women started coming to my house. They all gave me money and there's almost one hundred dollars here. We are unanimous, Pastor Miller, we don't want it spent on flowers. Please give it to your church to carry on its work."

Hundreds of tributes were made to my mother in those days following her death, but none was more moving than this.

My mother had a running conversation with the Lord throughout her life. Her prayer life was certainly her most remarkable and memorable trait. She had a sense of wonder that helped her be creative. And she had a sense of humor that helped her never to take herself too seriously. But it was definitely her prayer life that set her apart from all other women.

No one was left out of her praying. Immediate family, distant relatives, church members, PTA women, sorority women, children, teenagers, Bible class women, neighbors — *everyone* was prayed over.

I was particularly rich in that much of her praying was for me, and one of the things I miss most, now

88

that she's gone, is this aspect of her life which so encompassed me.

She'd phone me almost every morning of the last five years of her life. She'd wake me up with the words, "Good morning, honey! Well, tell me, what wonderful thing has God done for you today?"

"Oh, brother!" I'd groan. "Here I am not even fully awake yet and she wants to know *what exactly* has God done?" I was always forced into finding *something*, anything to praise the Lord about.

After she'd make the usual noises mothers make to daughters, she'd tell me what she was praying about that morning or what the Lord had told her, and· she'd reach into that huge Resource Account of hers and come up with one pearl of great price after another.

Two months before she died she phoned and after the usual "What's God done for you," she restated the question.

"Now, Joyce," she said emphatically, "I'm serious. What *has* the Lord done? I know He's really done something terrific!" She was very excited, and I was very blasé because I couldn't think of *anything* the Lord had done, much less something terrific.

"Now, I mean it — what's happened today?" she repeated.

"Nothing, mother, absolutely nothing."

"Did you get anything wonderful in the mail? Are you going to do some TV work? Is the broadcast syndicated?"

"Mother," I said wearily, "all I got in the mail yesterday and today were four bills and one rather negative letter from a radio listener of mine who thought I

89

said, 'creme de menthe liqueur' when I really said, 'This recipe takes creme-de-menthe-flavored sherbet.' And the answer to all those other questions is *no*.

She could barely believe me. "Are you positive?"

By now I was ready for some explanations, so she finally said, "Well, this morning when I was praying for you, the Lord told me He was going to open up a brand new ministry for you — something you've never done before and something that will reach thousands of people."

I laughed and said, "Well, not today, sweetie!" She ignored my flippancy and would not be dissuaded from her knowledge. She insisted that the Lord was working.

"Mark my words, dear daughter, on this day, the fifteenth of July, the Lord has opened a new ministry in your life!"

We talked some more and I ended our phone conversation by teasing her about how clouded her crystal ball was. She stubbornly refused to believe that "nothing" had happened.

Two weeks later, while I was at Biola College taping several weeks of radio programs, one of the secretaries handed me the large box of mail from listeners. Right on top was a letter from Floyd Thatcher who was then director of publications for Zondervan Publishing House.

As I read it I was absolutely stunned. I held it out to a secretary and said, "Hey, does this sound like a serious offer?"

She read it and said, "It sure does. He's seen your *King's Business* magazine articles and now wants you to consider writing a full-length manuscript — a book!"

I could hardly believe it — a world-famous publishing company asking *me* to write a book was too much. I wouldn't even have written for *King's Business* if I hadn't complained to the managing editor, Al Sanders, about it having no women's page. He responded with, "Fine, *you* write it!"

Coming home from Biola that day I found my parents had decided to surprise me with a visit. When the usual hugging and kissing was over I said, "Oh, mother, I've *got* to read you something!" And I dug the letter out of the box.

Cancer was beginning to whip her into its own form, so I sat on the edge of the couch where she was lying while I read Mr. Thatcher's letter. When I finished I said, "Well, what do you think of that, mother? Did you ever think your daughter would write a book?"

I still can see her so clearly. She never lifted her head at all but just lay there, smiled, and said very softly, "I *always* knew." Then she added just as quietly, "If you check the date on that letter, you'll probably see it's marked July 15."

It was.

God shared His thoughts, His plans, and His ideas with her at all hours and times. He revealed Himself to her in His Word as I've never seen before.

You can imagine then with this kind of praying mother, my utter shock and dismay when after her death, in one of her notebooks I found the heading, "When God Did Not Answer My Prayer."

They were almost the words of a heretic. She who believed God would do anything had suggested He

91

did not, or could not — I wasn't sure. Eagerly I read on.

Before you start reading her story, stop right here. Now, try to remember when you asked God for something and He didn't answer you. Or, ask yourself when was the last time you said either to yourself, God, or someone else, "I've prayed but God doesn't answer my prayers." Remember? Good, now go on.

She wrote:

"The time: early fall of 1931. I was pregnant with Joyce.

"Place: Oil fields of Michigan. In the home of the Pastor.

"Why: Three weeks of evangelistic meetings.

"Needs: Personal ones and this was the time of the depression.

"Outward appearance: I had one yellow and blue silk shantung two-piece dress. I got that before we were married. I did buy for my honeymoon a sample hat made of striped silk ribbon marked down from $8.00 to $4.00. I owned a white wool coat. (I bought that too before marriage.)

"Amount received per week: $7.50 (It took us $10.00 to get there.)

"Situation: While there for those weeks we lived with the pastor, shared his home, food, and hospitality. The frying pan was ready each morning from the day before. Potatoes were always fried in it. The coffee pot had grounds of yesterday's coffee and another spoonful of new coffee thrown in each morning. They just let it boil. The eggs swam in the grease. For lunch we had fried potatoes and beans from the same

92

greasy pan. Stewed tomatoes, and coffee from the same pot from breakfast. Supper was fried potatoes and beans again (from the same pan). Tomatoes, coffee, and, for variation, fried bacon with flour sprinkled on it.

"We coasted into Oil Fields, Michigan on our last gallon of gas and before too many days we wanted to get out if for nothing other than to change our menu for just one meal. We waited each night after the service to see if we'd get an offering, but found that no offering would be given until a love offering was taken at the end of our three weeks. We had to wait three weeks! Eternity seemed shorter.

"Usually the mail would bring us a dollar or two but each time the mail came it was just mail — no dollars. I prayed for just *one* dollar so we could go out and change our diet.

"Each morning, after the mail arrived, we would have prayer with the pastor and his wife. When the Pastor received mail with any money in it, he would wave it high above his head to the Lord and have a praise service and what he called a 'Jericho March,' thanking God as we all stomped around his living room (sort of a sanctified dance line). But there was no money in our mail.

"I went into the bedroom early one morning and petitioned Jesus to please send us just a dollar — just enough to get us to the nearest restaurant for a hamburger. (You could do this on a dollar in those days.) A real joy swept over me and I got up from my knees confident that my petitions were heard and that the answer was on the way! I encouraged my husband;

93

he, by now, had the making of several good-sized boils, but I assured him that God would send us mail on the morrow.

"He did! We opened our mail, but no money. My heart sank. Then God spoke and told me that He *would* give me the one dollar. The pastor, about that moment, opened his mail, sent up a shout, and waved a $10 bill. As plain as your voice, God spoke to me and said, 'He will give you 10 percent of his money as an offering.' So I, too, got in the hallelujah line and thanked Him for my dollar. But after the Jericho March I groaned as I saw him put the $10 back in his envelope. I never saw it or my dollar nor was there any mention of it — ever.

"I felt depressed and quite uncertain as to my assurance, His Word, and answered prayer. So I thought, *Well, maybe I'd better pray for a two-cent postage stamp so I can write my mother and ask her for a dollar.*

"I went into the bedroom and prayed in earnest for God to give me the desire of my heart and send me just one two-cent stamp. Again I had complete assurance that my prayer was answered.

"The next morning after our reliable fried potatoes breakfast we had devotions and then opened the mail.

"We got mail — but no stamps. But bless me! Pastor got happy, started his Jericho March and waved a *whole page* of two-cent stamps. You will get ten of those two-cent stamps,' the Lord said. I joined in the praise march for I was getting ten stamps instead of the one I'd asked for!

"But in horror I watched the pastor put the stamps

94

back in the envelope without a word or my ten stamps.

"This time I was really bewildered, confused, and doubts raced through my mind. I doubted particularly the power of prayer and made up my mind. It was not God assuring me. I'd never get a tenth of that ten dollars or the ten stamps — after all it was just all in my mind!

"Finally our three weeks were over and we left with our love offering and my husband's boils.

"*Later:* Times were hard, money scarce but we settled in Saginaw, Michigan, and there we received our training of wants and needs. Joyce was born, but as times were hard my heart grew harder. *I knew it didn't pay to pray* — even if I did, God didn't hear or care or even know my needs — let alone supply them!

"My weight dropped down to 89 pounds. I doubted God, I hated people for being selfish, I lived in bitterness within and hardship without. Our baby was sick and needed nourishment. It was a desperate time.

"Two years later, my husband was called to assist a pastor in Dearborn, Michigan, for one week. To supply his own church in Saginaw, he invited an evangelist to fill his pulpit. He had them stay in our home.

"It happened that one day after I had gone through a form of prayer and family worship, a discussion began about God's answers to prayer.

"I felt I had to let the fountains of the deep break open in my heart and I poured out to the evangelist's wife my experiences in Oil Fields, Michigan. I told her I could never feel I would ever be assured of answered prayer again.

95

"I thought the tears that fell down her cheeks were in pity for me, but not so — she had a story to tell me. She and her husband had just come from two weeks of meetings with that very pastor and our names were mentioned. The pastor had spit these words out. 'The Millers are proud people and very rich. Why she had silk dresses, a hat, and a beautiful white coat. He had a good car and do you know, we were poor, yet we had to feed them, and they never offered to buy a thing for the table? They were stuck up and fancy! Why, once I got money through the mail and I thought, *I'll share with them one dollar as a tithe*, but then I thought, *No, why should I? They have more than we do!* Why, a day or so later I even thought I'd give them ten stamps I got in the mail, but then I thought, *They should give me stamps, not I; they are selfish and better off than I!*' I listened and was just stunned.

"What really hit me as I listened was that God *had* heard my prayer! He *had* spoken to the instrument that was to give the answer. But the individual heard the voice of God saying, 'Share ten percent of your blessings with the Millers,' and a big 'No!' was sent right back to God. 'Give ten stamps to the Millers,' God commands.

"'Why should I?' he counters. 'They're better off than I!'"

"God spoke to my heart through this experience. He answers prayers through *you* and me. He does not drop dollars from the sky like rain, nor hang stamps on the trees like fruit — this is contrary to His laws. *You* fulfill and answer His prayers by being touched

96

and moved to give to God's work and God's children.

"I promised God that day that when I pray and no answer comes, after self-examination and being sure of no hindering sin, my prayer will be, "Dear Jesus, *thank* You, Lord, for *hearing* my prayer. I know it's not You who fails — I'll wait till another hears Your voice and answers Your will and commands."

My mother learned this lesson well, early in her marriage. Prayer became her most beautiful contribution to those who knew her.

All through her life, from that time on, she responded to even the faintest suggestion from the Holy Spirit. She did not want to be guilty of failing to be God's instrument in answering someone's prayer.

I remember many times she visited someone, and it became the turning point for them. Or, she would write someone a letter at the precise moment they needed it. She was just as generous with her money as with her time.

In the last year of her life, she had a little fund started in an envelope for a pair of white summer shoes. She'd been thinking about a pair of white pumps for just months. One Sunday she had five dollars in her little envelope. As she walked into church, the Lord said, "Give those five dollars to Bill over there."

She only hesitated for a second and, muttering something about, "Okay, Lord, so there go my shoes," she gave the five dollars to the young man. We now know that that simple act of kindness was the turning point for a financially desperate young man. That God would answer on the spot his prayer for five dollars was utterly incredible to him. His faith in God would never again drop so low because of Mother's pressing those five dollars into his hand.

The next morning Mother opened her mail and the Lord said, "Now, Marion, about those shoes you wanted" — and out of a letter fell ten dollars. A friend had written, "I just wanted you to have this!"

After some thirty years of trusting and praying she wrote, "Christians today, as always, are waiting on God to answer their prayers. Many have waited long and have doubted God has heard. Others have become offended especially when God has said, 'No' (or worse yet, 'Not now') and have charged God foolishly. When Job's whole life went out the window the Scripture says, 'In all this Job did not sin or charge God with wrong' (Job 1:22, RSV).

"God's waiting room is the most tiresome and unpleasant place in our Christian experience. We do not like delays or denials, for hasn't God said, 'Ask, and it shall be given you' (Matt. 7:7)? God has reasons for delays. Some He will reveal to us, others we may never know, but one thing we know for certain — God *never* makes a mistake!"

I cannot write about this lovely mother of mine without using the word faith. In her writings "prayer" and "faith" are so entangled that you don't find one without the other.

She wrote: "God has established the law of prayer and faith. Prayer is being conscious of need — while faith supplies it.

"Prayer never obtains anything from God unless faith is present and active. Faith never receives anything from God unless prayer makes a petition. Prayer and faith work harmoniously together — both are necessary in their distinct function, but they are quite different in their nature.

"Prayer is the voice of the soul, while faith is the hand. It is only through prayer that the soul can establish communion with the Creator, and it is only through faith that spiritual victories are won. Prayer knocks at the door of grace, while faith opens it. Prayer contacts God, while faith obtains an audience. Prayer makes a petition, while faith presses through the multitude to touch the hem of His garment and receive from His giving hand. Prayer quotes the promises, while faith boldly proclaims the fulfillment of that promise!"

Mother lived her more than fifty years on prayer and faith. This Resource Account is mine because of her.

My mother was wealthy beyond words. An heir of God! I found one paragraph that sums her up completely. This is her personal testimony — her statement of faith.

"When God found me, I was no better than a cobblestone — hardly worth picking up. But He took me into His laboratory of grace, and by the chemistry of atoning blood, He processed me, and I came out as His jewel — a bit rough, I'll admit, but after a few years of cutting, buffing, and polishing, He will present me at last before His throne, and I shall be absolutely flawless. Miraculous though it be, it is true that God, through the power of the Cross, can transform you into a precious jewel.

"What a joy it is to go through life knowing that we are among heaven's gems and 'In That Day' when He makes up His jewels — *we* shall be included!"

Mother prayed when she felt like it, when she didn't feel like it, when it was easy, and when it was hard. She prayed when she cooked supper, when she gardened, (several times neighbors caught her talking to her roses), when she vacuumed, while she read, and as she listened to thousands of people pour out their hearts to her.

She was not some religious nut who went around mumbling to herself all the time — she simply talked to God as easily as she breathed. When you talked with her you knew *He* was listening in too.

Every time I meet someone who is really on speaking terms with God, as my mother was, I am surprised to find their time spent in praying and studying God's Word is *always longer* than mine!

We long to own a *sensational* prayer-answering service, but we don't bother to keep up the payments, so the Lord repossesses our prayer life, and we stand around wondering how we lost it.

My mother knew how to pray as some people play the piano, *by ear*. I am always amused when someone asks me to *show* them how I play by ear. It's impossible — try as I may I can't explain how I have *always* been able to hear a song once and then play it.

It was the same with Mother and her praying. Not long ago I heard a series of messages on prayer by Dr. Curtis Mitchell, Professor of Bible at Biola College. I was amazed at the similarity of his views on prayer (which he had developed after a considerable study of the prayers of Jesus and the disciples) to my mother's views.

It was thrilling to hear Dr. Mitchell say, "Our responsibility is to *ask!* God's responsibility is to *do!*"

He captured the essence of mother's prayer life when he spoke about the act of prayer. He said, "Prayer is an act of specific requests." Jesus was always specific in what He prayed for. Dr. Mitchell went on to tell that in his own prayer life the more *unconcerned* he was, the more general his prayers. When he was deeply *concerned*, his prayers were completely specific. That was my mother's secret in her prayer life — very specific requests!

She was so concerned — honestly, sincerely concerned for people, things, and even rose bushes that looked a little puny — that she always prayed *specifically*. She gave God every opportunity to answer specifically, and *He did!*

One other interesting pattern in mother's specific prayer life was that she petitioned God for some *material* need about 10 percent of the time, but 90 percent of the time was for the *spiritual* need of herself, her family, or a friend or acquaintance. At many of the prayer meetings I've been in the percentage was completely reversed — 90 percent asking God for material help or physical help and only 10 percent asking for spiritual needs.

We all have this Resource Account available to us. It was not just some extraordinary gift God *only* gave to my mother. Her only edge was that many times she had no place to go, no one to talk to, nowhere to turn to except the Lord — *so she did!* She did it with all

101

the doors of her soul opened wide to the risk of loving others through Christ.

She appropriated the power of the Holy Spirit and used the Resource Account to its fullest extent!

You can too!

The Refinement Account

The Refinement Account

Our dog Popotla, we call him Popo for convenience, has a problem. Actually, he has several problems, but the one I'd like to tell you about is a problem named August the Ninth. August was just a six-week-old yellow kitten when our daughter, Laurie, compassionately brought him home to live with us.

Popo took one look at that little butterball of yellow fur, and, even though he towered above the kitten, he was *terrified*. The kitten was actually delighted to see Popo. *Just another larger-type cat*, he thought. He immediately wanted to show his friendliness and would have been delighted to have romped all day, except that Popo went into the first stages of a nervous breakdown — he withdrew to the corner and cried a lot.

In the weeks to follow I stopped a lot of activities to watch as that tiny ball of yellow fur reduced a good-sized dog into a whimpering, simpering, neurotic mess.

August chased him. Popo ran. August touched him. Popo shook. August pounced and attacked him. Popo jumped. August clung to his throat. Popo walked around with this "thing" swinging gently under his chin.

In short, Popo had *quite* a problem, and as I saw it, he had three options:

1. He could get mad. He could get absolutely vicious and kill that cat. I called the veterinarian who knows Popo and asked how much stronger the dog was than the kitten. "Immensely," the doctor said. "That dog could lift one paw and by setting it squarely on August could snuff him out like a small candle."

Had Popo been able to talk, he might have said to us, "How *dare* you do this to me?" Or, "How could you, a loving family, say you love me and at the same time give me this problem?" He really had a genuine right never to trust us again. Yet he did not choose to get mad or lose his faith.

2. His second option was to ignore the cat completely. He could have gritted his teeth, admirably controlled his panic, and walked around like there *was no August the Ninth.* We would have admired that noble attitude even if ignoring a problem isn't too realistic. But Popo chose a third option.

3. He admitted he *did* have a problem. He decided that since August seemed destined to stay forever, he'd be thankful for him and *accept* him. For the first time since the kitten had started chasing him, Popo stopped, turned slowly around and faced the enemy straight on. August had never before seen this tactic and wasn't too prepared for Popo's paw that playfully knocked all four feet out from under him. After that it was fun and games for both of them. Once in a while the kitten got the best or worst end, but it was usually

106

pretty well even. Now, after some months, they are able to sleep side by side in gentle peace.

I don't know what convinced Popo to tackle his problem head on, but he seemed to have the problem under control after he'd restructured his own attitude. After acknowledging his problem, he began to *accept* it. He took the third option and I was delighted by his decision. I was also aware of something strangely human about this situation.

Most of us, when faced with problems, refuse in one way or another to *accept* them and many times we take the first option — *anger*.

Not too long ago I received a traffic ticket for following too closely. The policeman, as he handed me my copy of the citation, thanked me for being co-operative. He mistook my silence for cooperation. Actually, I was furious with the whole situation and didn't dare open my mouth for fear I'd spend the night in jail. It was the last straw in a very bad day! I was tired from singing in a recording session, it was late at night, and I had been trying to pass a lady in a winding canyon because *her* driving was so erratic. *She* should have gotten the ticket! I was angry with everything that night and particularly at the personal injustice dealt to me, and even though I didn't lose my temper, I certainly could not come up with one reason as to why the whole thing had happened.

David Augsburger, in his fabulous book on forgiveness,* talks about Jesus' anger and he says, "His anger was over principles of right and wrong, not over per-

* *Seventy Times Seven* (Moody Press, 1970).

sons and personalities. Christ's anger was never motivated by personal abuse."

My anger that night was most certainly motivated by what I felt was personal abuse! I was angry at God, too, because all day I'd been about His work, and I was tired and spent when this happened.

We often wonder, *Why did this happen to me? Why is God doing this to me?*

Is it wrong to become angry about our problems? Yes, I sincerely believe that when we choose to get angry over the situations that bother us we have chosen the wrong option.

The night I got the ticket I should have said, "Okay, Lord, what are You going to teach me from this one?" Later I'll share what happened the day I showed up in court to pay my fine.

The second option is to ignore the whole situation as if that will make it go away.

As long as we are alive and breathing, we will have problems. Only the dead are finished with the daily problems of life. Someone suffered pain to give you birth, someone will go through unbearable pain when you die, and all the time between these two events there will be pain. Pain is a part of living.

My pastor, Ted Cole, talks frequently about our contemporary heartaches, sufferings, and disappointments and he always refers to them as "heaven-sent refinements."

God uses the pain, the failures, and the hurts of our lives as tools to help us grow spiritually. But we often prefer to resent or ignore situations.

108

Our third option is to accept and use problems. That's God's solution, but it's a tough assignment.

I find myself falling right in line with tens of thousands of people who, when a problem presents itself, want *out, out, out!* I don't like rain on my parades, lumps in my gravy, or dirty-diapered babies. The first thing I come up with is, "How can I solve this problem?"

What astounds me about my attitude toward problems is that it is *completely opposed* to what is presented in the Bible.

When James says to me in his first chapter, ". . . is your life full of difficulties and temptations? Then be happy" (v. 2, *Living Bible*). I think, *Oh, come on, Brother James, are you kidding? Be happy when my washer breaks down? Especially since the washer always feels the need of a comrade, so the stove or water heater joins the strike against me at exactly the same moment?*

Then James rubs salt in the wound when he says, ". . . and don't try to squirm out of your problems" (v. 4, *Living Bible*). Actually, I find I'm very happy about problems when I am squirming *out* of them, rather than sloshing around in them.

James is truly convinced that these troubles will make us grow. I'm not sure I want to — not quite that much anyway — because growing always hurts.

How can I accept the problems of living and how can I be happy during the refining process? How does anyone do that?

I think acceptance begins with thanking and prais-

109

ing the Lord *immediately* for the situation, person, or conflict.

If you read the following verses to a group of Christian women, they'll agree wholeheartedly with them: "No matter what happens, always be joyful, for this is God's will for you who belong to Christ Jesus" (1 Thess. 5:18, *Living Bible*); "And we know that all that happens to us is working for our good if we love God and are fitting into his plans" (Rom. 8:28, *Living Bible*).

They will agree that we should *always* be joyful, we should *always* pray, and we should *always* thank God. They will agree that God controls even the minutest detail of our lives and that all of it works together! They all, to a woman, agree that these words are true *except when they are in trouble.* When they hear the doctor say, "cancer," when their child dies, when their best friend breaks their confidence, when their husband loses his job, then these same Christian women fall apart just like their non-Christian neighbors.

I can be hard on these hypothetical women because I've been caught in the same trap many times. I thoroughly believe I'm to be joyful and really thank God for everything *until* something goes wrong. Then I do not "in everything give thanks," but rather I say, "Oh, why Lord? Why me?" It's a natural reflex.

I've been going to prayer meetings for years, yet I've never heard:

"Thank You, Lord, my son just got his draft notice."

"Thank You, Lord, this morning my husband and I had that same fight about the toothpaste tube."

"Thank You, Lord, my daughter did not win the essay contest."

110

"Thank You, Lord, my husband was just fired."

"Thank You, Lord, the TV set broke, the washer broke, and we just found out our son has to have braces on his teeth."

"Thank You, Lord, the doctor told me today I have lung cancer."

"Thank You, Lord, my Christian boss has just cheated me out of two months' salary."

"Thank You, Lord, my wife just asked me for a divorce."

"Thank You, Lord, my husband has to have surgery."

And certainly not once in my life have I stood up and said, "I thank the Lord I have a husband who asks me every night of my life, 'Joyce, have you locked the back door?' and, after I say 'Yes,' gets up and checks it."

No, I've never thanked the Lord for that. And believe me, the night I got the ticket I never thought of thanking *anyone*, much less the Lord.

I could go on, but I think you can see the list is endless. I've never, in all my years of being in or out of church, heard these thank you's, yet God tells us in *everything* to give thanks.

David, the psalmist, was really convinced that if problems and thankfulness were companions life would take on new dimensions.

He wrote, "It is good to say, 'Thank You' to the Lord, to sing praises to the God who is above all gods. Every morning tell him, 'Thank you for your kindness,' and every evening rejoice in all his faithfulness" (Ps. 92:1, 2, *Living Bible*).

Later, when things evidently were looking worse,

he wrote, "I will praise the Lord *no matter what happens*" (Ps. 34:1, *Living Bible*).

Why don't we hear thanks to the Lord *no matter what happens?* Is it because bad things never happen to God's people? Oh, no! Trouble, sickness, and disappointment fall on Christians and non-Christians alike. No one is immune from trouble. The reason we don't hear these thank you's is that few Christians *really* believe those verses except when everything is fine.

So hundreds of thousands of Christians go from one defeat to another because they find praising and thanking God impossible when things go wrong.

I've read many books on thanking the Lord and they have touched me deeply — for a time. Why is it that for awhile at least, I'm stirred to thank God and then I forget? I wonder, will I ever come to the point of total commitment where, no matter *what* happens, I'll be so sure God is controlling each factor that I'll spontaneously thank Him for everything?

It was while we were vacationing in Mexico this summer that I realized why I don't thank God for the bad as well as the good.

With another family we share the joys of a little "casa" on the Pacific Ocean. Its remote Mexican charm always gentles our spirit. However, it does have *very* faulty plumbing.

This year when I heard my husband yell, "Oh, for Pete's sake — not again!" I knew the toilet had come apart at the seams the third time *that day*. Now here was a real down-to-earth problem.

It wasn't directly *my* problem so I could be quite objective and even a little smug as I called to Dick,

"Honey, in view of what we've been learning about thanking God for our problems, do you think you could say, 'Thank You, Lord, the toilet has broken again'?"

"No, Joyce, I don't think I'm spiritually up to it at this point!"

His answer really hit me — isn't that where we all live? Our spiritual batteries are charged up by some book or speaker and we burn brightly with enthusiastic gratitude. But as time passes we dwindle down from brightness to twilight and "spiritually we're not up to it" when the problems arrive.

It's so easy to thank the Lord for all the good, beautiful things. Just that week we had said in all sincerity, "Thank You, Lord, for the safe, fun trip down into Mexico."

"Thank You, Lord, for the beautiful ocean and the marvelous brown pelicans that put on soaring flight demonstrations each day."

"Thank You, Lord, for the delicious food."

But in all the years we've been going down to that casa, I've never heard anyone say, "Thank You, Lord, we just ran out of butane gas for the stove and fridge."

"Thank You, Lord, for all that gooey tar that washed up on the beach and it's clinging to everyone's feet."

And certainly I've never heard anyone say, "Thank You, Lord, it's *my* turn to do the dishes!"

The morning after Dick had fixed the plumbing we had finished devotions and began talking about thanking God. Dick voiced his feelings by saying he really didn't know what good was accomplished if I had been able to thank God for the broken toilet.

"Oh, but honey, because of thanking God two

113

things happened," I said. "When the plumbing was restored I was very glad the stupid thing conked out because it made me appreciate *working* plumbing; and secondly, the thought that my banker executive husband fixed it was a deep source of pride and satisfaction to me!" We both smiled. It was no big deal, no big spiritual revelation — or was it? Some of the most difficult things to thank the Lord for are the unexpected, small, annoying problems. But even worse are the unfair and unjust things.

One of the most unjust situations I've ever known involved a nineteen-year-old college girl named Sue.

In the early spring of this year she phoned me, and before she had finished saying hello, it was obvious she was utterly devastated.

I asked her what in the world was wrong. She poured out in detail a conversation she had just had with her father. Sue's mother had died a few years before and her father had remarried. For some unexplainable reason he had phoned her, and told her casually that she was now on her own. His words had hit her like a ton of bricks. She was incredulous. He had gone on to say that she was no longer his responsibility. She was to make her own decisions and, since he had no place for her during the coming summer months, she was to make her own plans.

She was sobbing and mumbling something about how unfair it was when she heard her father tell her that after all, *he* had been on his own, working and shifting for himself, when he was nineteen. He implied that it was simply a normal thing. Long after he

114

hung up she remained at the phone, utterly crushed and completely broken-hearted.

At first I was furious with her father. I knew this girl to be one of the most talented, lovable, conscientious students alive. She was truly given to being God's girl. How could her father say such thoughtless, cruel things?

I immediately remembered a scene from my past. Once, long after I had grown up, I was visiting my mother and was pouring out some minor problems when suddenly I stopped and said, "Oh, mother, I'm sorry to be burdening you with these problems. I'm a big girl. I'm on my own now and I shouldn't bother you."

She reacted immediately and said in her sternest voice, "My dear girl, I don't care how old you get or how many years you are married, you will always be my girl, and you will never have to be on your own!"

The memory of that moment warmed me, but I could not share it with this broken-hearted girl; it would have made the contrast too great. Then I thought of Dick's father. Even though he is in his 70's and Dick has been on his own for years, if we ever knocked on dad's door and said, "We have nothing — we've lost everything. Can we come in and live with you?" the door would be flung open with no questions asked, and we would know we were not on our own! I couldn't share this with the girl either.

"Oh, God," I prayed, "here I am — furious at her father and I can't be any help at all with this ugly spirit in me. Help me to love and give thanks for this inconsiderate man and give me the right words to

115

bind and heal her crushed heart." I found myself talking about the verse "honor thy father and thy mother." I reminded Sue that it does not say we are to honor them because they are smart, or right, or beautiful, or anything else, but because they are our father and mother.

I recalled vividly an illustration Ken Poure had given to a group of high school kids at Hume Lake on this very verse. At another meeting he had been speaking about honoring parents. After the meeting a girl came up to him and said, "I can't honor my parents — and I never will be able to." When he asked why, she told him this story.

Her parents had divorced and the courts awarded her and her three brothers to the mother for six months of the year and then to the father for the next six months. They had spent the first six months with the mother and then eagerly traveled, with the sister driving, to another part of the country to begin the next months with their father. When she found the house, they spotted their father on the porch across the street. The boys were so anxious to see their father that without thinking or looking they jumped out of the car, ran across the street, were hit by a car, and were all killed. The young girl said to Ken, "I'll get over their deaths in time. That isn't what really bothers me. What really gets me is this: I can never honor my mother and father because neither one of them attended my brothers' funeral." Then God gave Ken the wisdom to tell this girl that perhaps she was the strong girl she was because of this very thing, that perhaps God had allowed this inexplicable, unfair,

116

unjust thing to happen to make her into God's chosen vessel. This had been her time of refinement.

I related this story to the distraught young girl on the phone. I said, "If you can allow yourself to learn from this experience, to even *thank God* for this father who has treated you unjustly — who knows what can be accomplished by it? How do you know but what this is the very making of you?"

Since this girl was of such sterling character, she quickly got hold of herself, looked firmly at the facts, and, although she understood none of her father's words, at that very moment she began to thank God. Acceptance had begun.

Now I wish that I could say that two weeks later God honored Sue's faith and that her father apologized deeply for his words, took her into his arms, and asked her forgiveness. But as a matter of fact, things did not get better, they got much worse.

As the semester drew to a close Sue's stepmother asked her what she would be doing during the summer. She said she could qualify at a distant university for courses during the summer or stay at the college and get a job. Her stepmother responded, "Good, because you can't stay with us. We don't have any room."

Hot tears filled Sue's eyes and her thoughts centered on, "They don't want me. They don't have any room for me. I am alone. Nobody wants me."

I saw her a few hours later. There she was, thanking God for this new hurt. She stayed in our living room that whole night, and once more the Lord brought joy in the morning. For the next few days He sent the balm of Gilead to soothe her troubled, wounded heart. His presence made up for the lack of parents and parental love. He surrounded her. The growing made her glow with beauty! Her time of refinement was showing.

The next few weeks were really wonderful. God gave Sue not one, but two sets of loving foster parents. They spent the summer lavishing on her all the love and prayers that could be showered on her. She did more exciting, marvelous things in this summer of her life than ever before. She even managed several university courses and collected some needed credits. This would be enough to write about because God healed every large wound and every small cut. It all began with thanking Him for such an unjust thing. But this is only a small part of what God accomplished that summer.

One day while she was attending summer classes, Sue felt led to stay in the dorm, even though she had never before cut classes. A kitten ran into Sue's dorm room, made a circle, and ran scampering out. She chased it down the hall, and, before she knew it, the kitten had bounced into an open doorway, and she found herself in another woman's room. The woman was working on some papers, looked up, and recognized the girl. "Oh, honey," she said, "I've seen you before and I've been wanting to get better acquainted with you! Sit down."

The conversation was easy, the woman gracious. Then, as in so many other Spirit-led discussions, the woman asked the girl to tell her about her background. The young girl sat there and innocently shared her life and her mother's death. Then, and only God knows

118

why, she shared her father's rejection and the telephone conversation she'd had with me. By the time Sue had neared the finish, the woman was starting to cry. Little by little the tears changed to sobbing.

"How old are you?" the woman asked between sobs.

"I'm nineteen," Sue answered.

Taking Sue's hand, the stranger told of her background. In her case, her father had died, and her mother had rejected her. She told of her inability to accept or honor her mother. She tearfully confessed that she was fifty years old, the wife of a minister, and had never been able to face the facts and forgive her mother or thank God. She was filled with wonder that this girl, at nineteen, could have learned such a lesson. But of course, we know the terrible price it took. The decision to thank God in everything costs us a great price, but it brings priceless dividends. The conversation between these two was the turning point for the older woman.

There is not a shadow of doubt in my mind that Sue's rejection by her father was the making of the girl. God used her biggest heartache to the maximum amount of good some six months later. I believe it was all locked up the moment Sue, so many months back, began to praise God.

"Happy are those who have suffered persecution for the cause of goodness, for the kingdom of Heaven is theirs" (Matt. 5:10, Phillips' translation). Colleen Evans said of that verse, "Happy is the woman who can be unjustly criticized without jumping to her own defense." Happy, too, is the woman who can endure the most unfair treatment of all and not only accept it, but say, "Thank You, God, for this awful thing!" This woman is really rich! If the kingdom of heaven is this woman's, think of the real estate value tied up in her.

I know, firsthand, of one young college girl and one fifty-year-old woman who, because of thanking God for an extremely unjust thing, are immensely wealthy!

We all have the option of getting angry with God and shouting, "Why are You doing this to me?" But how much richer we can be if we learn to say, "Lord, what do You want me to learn from it?"

We can ignore our problems and say they don't really exist. But acknowledging that the problem is ours and then *before* the smoke has cleared away, thanking God for it, there's an experience!

Can you write down the problem that really is bugging you the most right now? After examining it to see if you need to be forgiven or to *give* forgiveness, can you write, "Thank You, Lord, for this problem?" If you can, one of the first things that will happen is the tense, tied-up feeling you have will relax. Why shouldn't it? Doesn't God know all about the broken washer or the cancer surgery? If He knows about it, then He knows the ending too. Can you trust Him with it today?

I can, and it's much easier to bear today when I've begun it by thanking Him. The bitterness lifts and my mind clears so much that the problem, while it doesn't go away, is easily put into the right perspective.

A military wife in Hawaii was complaining to me about her terrible quarters. She described the kind of housing she had left at the last post and how let down she was about this new housing. In particular, the kitchen was a disaster area. I looked at her over lunch and said, "Dot, do you think you could thank God for that crummy kitchen?"

Well, she wasn't too eager and showed no confidence that she'd be able to do such a strange thing. But some weeks after I came home I received this note from her. It said, "My kitchen is not *nearly* as crummy as I thought, thanks to your visit to Hawaii." I could almost see her shoulders relax.

I wish I'd been closer to the Lord the night I got that traffic ticket. Physically it wouldn't have worked such a hardship on my nervous system, and mentally it wouldn't have scrambled my thoughts so badly. Had I been able to thank God, the whole situation would have been exciting. God had quite a plan in mind that night.

Three weeks later I went to court. I had to pay my almost-thirty-dollar fine in person, so I decided to talk with the judge. By then, I was able to thank the Lord even though I really didn't think the whole thing was fair. I'll never forget the experience.

After I told my sad story to the judge (he cut my fine in half), I realized with a jolt that this was the same courtroom and the same judge who held the trial for the men who had kidnapped and robbed Dick some three years before. °

I told him about my book and the story in it and asked if I could give him a copy. We had a wonderful talk together and he told me he would read the whole book.

° See Prologue to *His Stubborn Love* (Zondervan Publishing House, 1971).

THE RICHEST LADY IN TOWN

I went out to the car and brought back a copy of *His Stubborn Love.* By that time the courtroom was filled so I simply walked to the clerk's counter.

Before I could say anything, six women clerks charged up to me and said, "Is that the book? What's it about?"

"Well, it's about a marriage that was finished and a God who gave a new marriage back to the same old people," I answered.

These six women and one judge all read the witness of God's love.

I could never have waltzed in there and said, "Hey, you needy people with such big marital problems, have I got a book for you!" Instead, God gave me a traffic ticket, but typically, I didn't thank Him or accept it until much later.

God wants to do many marvelous things with the problems He gives us, and He alone knows *which* problems and how many you, personally, can stand or need.

The Refinement Account is one few of us want to draw from, yet once experienced, it is a lesson for which we wouldn't take a million dollars.

Peter wrote, "After you have suffered a little while, our God, who is full of kindness through Christ, will give you his eternal glory. He personally will come and pick you up, and set you firmly in place, and make you stronger than ever" (1 Peter 5:10, *Living Bible*).

You can draw from this account, you can even accept it and be grateful for it because *our God* has noted each deposit and withdrawal during our troubled, painful times, and He "will come and pick you up, and set you firmly in place, and make you stronger [richer?] than ever."

Stronger than ever? Yes, that's the result of refinement.

David knew a great deal about this account. He wrote,

> Let all who are discouraged take heart. Let us praise the Lord together, and exalt his name.
>
> For I cried to him and he answered me! He freed me from all my fears. Others too were radiant at what he did for them. Theirs was no downcast look of rejection! This poor man cried to the Lord — and the Lord heard him and saved him out of his troubles. For the Angel of the Lord guards and rescues all who reverence him.
>
> Oh, put God to the test and see how kind he is! See for yourself the way his mercies shower down on all who trust in him. If you belong to the Lord, reverence him; for everyone who does this has everything he needs (Ps. 34:2-9, *Living Bible*).

Notice that God did not first of all free David from all his troubles but from all his fears.

If you draw from the Refinement Account, you'll know firsthand about the angels guarding and rescuing you, the mercies of God showering down on you, and having everything you need.

What an account! It's really a blank check, just waiting to be signed.

The Millionaires Account

The Millionaires Account

This book wouldn't be complete if I wrote only about *my* wealth, and certainly I should not give you the impression that the title, *The Richest Lady in Town,* refers only to me. Actually, it includes hundreds of Christian women who are daily exploring all the riches found in this exciting, captivating life.

I've probably left out other valuable accounts, but I must not leave out this chapter — the one about my millionaire friends. I am blessed with many millionaire friends. There's Bettye, Clare, Charlotte, Virginia, Ruth, Beverly, Eleanor, Martene, Judy, and many more; but let me zero in on just a few.

You probably know someone like them, and maybe after reading about my friends you'll understand what it is *exactly* that makes that certain friend of yours so priceless!

These friends all lead different lives and their life styles vary, but they all share one priceless ingredient: forgiveness.

It's not just that they have been forgiven, but all of them have *accepted* that lovely forgiveness. They have seen clearly the plain fact that God *did* forgive

127

them as He said He would, even though He knew every ugly, disappointing quality about them. Having accepted this forgiveness, they are free to forgive and accept others and the circumstances of life, no matter how great or horrible they might be.

Forgiveness shines and glows like a soft halo of light around each of these women. They have all taken Paul's words seriously when he wrote, "Be gentle and ready to forgive; never hold grudges. Remember, the Lord forgave you, so you must forgive others" (Col. 3: 13, *Living Bible*).

In *Seventy Times Seven* David Augsburger describes forgiveness as *rare*, hard, and costly. As you read about my millionaire friends, you will see just how rare, hard, and sometimes costly forgiveness is, and yet how marvelously rich these women are!

One of these friends is a fabulous minister's wife named Perky. I met her many years ago when I was the speaker for her church's mother-daughter banquet. I was naturally seated at the head table next to the minister's wife.

From almost the first minute I turned to meet her, I loved her. I was dazzled by her welcoming smile and gorgeous brown eyes. I had been tired when I came, but she refreshed my spirit so much that I'm sure I floated home instead of driving. She was the exact opposite of the minister's wife I'd been with the evening before. I'd spent a miserable time trying to talk to a depressing woman who hated her husband in general and her husband's ministry in particular.

All through childhood I had a chance to observe ministers' wives as they came through my dad's church and our parsonage. Then as God has allowed me to speak and sing in thousands of churches in the past ten or so years, I've met and talked with many more. Many of them were well-adjusted and happy, but even more were unhappy or even bitter.

Some of the problems of ministers' wives stem from the constant moving from one church to another and living in dreary parsonages which, if furnished, are filled with Sister Brown's choice castoffs and painted by Deacon Smith who never did know the difference between baby blue and navy blue.

Other problems arise because ministers' wives are often expected to be perfect. Someone, a long time ago, started the legend that ministers' wives, since they are married to "God's answer man," should be totally free from earthly problems, should be mature enough to take all suggestions, hints, and constructive criticism, and her children's behavior should border on saintly obedience.

Pity the poor wife who has any doubts or fears or suffers occasionally from a very human ailment called discouragement. And especially pity her if her child misbehaves, particularly *during* church! For then she will be told how to correct, handle, and rise above everything by any number of well-meaning folks.

Long after I was grown, my mother asked my forgiveness for "some things" she had done during my childhood.

"What things?" I asked.

Then she told me of the national magazine photographer who had seen us in a department store and asked if he could photograph me for their cover.

129

Mother told him yes and set up the appointment for the following Monday. On Sunday a woman in dad's church felt "led of the Lord" to point out all sorts of sins connected with the portrait such as, cameras and movies were alike, money would be given to the preacher's wife, etc. On it went, so mother cancelled the session.

When I asked her what she would have done differently had she had a second chance to be a minister's wife, she simply responded, "With every decision I had to make as a wife and mother I'd prayerfully go to the Lord and His Word. Then if I were sure I was not breaking any of His laws, I'd do whatever I, not Mrs. So-and-so, felt best."

Many congregations put the pastor's wife and children up on pillars with unrealistic and unobtainable standards. They have asked and expected far too much of them as human beings. However, wives and children of the preacher (myself included) have brought a great deal on themselves.

My friend Perky is free from all hang-ups and negative reactions in being a minister's wife. She is a pure, enthusiastic, brown-eyed joy!

Recently when I was under the dryer at the hairdresser's she tapped on the top of my hot metal dome and asked, "Hey, what are you writing so intently?"

"Oh, it's our anniversary. We've been married seventeen years and instead of a card, I'm writing Dick a letter. It's entitled 'Seventeen Reasons Why I'm Glad I Married Dick Landorf.'"

She was inspired by this bit of news, and, without any feelings of guilt, she stole my idea and wrote her own list for their anniversary. She called it, "Sixteen Reasons Why I'm Glad To Be Called Mrs. Brandt." Here are some of those reasons:

"1. Because I like sharing the name of not merely a 'big' person, but a 'great' person!

"2. I like the intimacy of hanging my toothbrush next to yours — even though you won't go modern with the electric one.

"3. And, frankly, I like the 'cut of your jib and the swing of your rudder' (especially in that gorgeous blue suit you reluctantly bought!).

"4. Who else can find a man *really involved* with other people and their problems who maintains a ready supply of humor constantly bubbling beneath the surface — just eager for an opportunity to spring forth!

"5. And who can find a man who is such a patient listener and wise counselor, yet loquacious enough to 'fill in' awkward silences!

"6. And when you face *my* shortcomings with humor and put them last on the list of 'important' things in life, as though they were all so minor, it does make it easier for me to accept *myself!*

"7. I admire your courage and willingness to tackle the unknown — all of life is an adventure with you!

"8. It's a rare man who continues to treat his wife like a queen long after courtship, but after sixteen years, the acid-test of marriage has not tarnished your exquisite manners.

"9. I'm glad you don't consider marriage a 50-50 partnership, even though we've agreed it's a 70-70

131

proposition. It seems like you're giving more than half *most* of the time! (I'm sure the children will always remember the times you do their dishes for them. When I walk in and exclaim what a good job they've done, you never tell me *you* did it. They look just as guilty as Al Capone's auditor!)

"10. I adore being your wife because it doesn't seem to threaten your masculinity to show compassion, especially toward your family. (You know, those spontaneous 'love taps' just make my day!)

"11. Yes, I can hold my head high when someone says, 'Are you *Mrs.* Donald Brandt?' because that name stands for truth, courage, and joy from one who has an adept way of spreading it!"

You see, Perky is quite wealthy! Part of it stems from the fact that her husband is not the *only* one "called of God." She has heard, clearly, the precious call of her husband to the ministry and has listened as God has softly called her to be the "preacher's wife" and then with all her might and soul has responded Yes!

In their years of marriage she has had to forgive her husband for accepting the call of God. Does that sound strange to you? It shouldn't, for we find sometimes, in the nitty-gritty of life we have to forgive others for good things as well as bad. One of the biggest things she's had to forgive and accept is that their house is on one end of the church parking lot and, any day of the week, twenty-five to thirty people will drop in. And that right there gives her twenty-five or thirty reasons to forgive her husband for being a minister.

Another friend of mine worth looking at because I'm made wealthy by her is my sister, Marilyn. She continues to add, year after year, to my supply of wealth.

She is very beautiful inside and out — so much so that the student body of Azusa Pacific College elected her their 1971 homecoming queen.

The day after her crowning I sat with her at the homecoming football game. She looked so beautiful and I was so proud of her. She is twenty years younger than I and only a year and a half older than our son, Rick, so I rarely think of her as my sister. It's always "Marilyn, my other child" and even more so since the death of our mother a few years ago.

My twenty-six-year-old brother, Cliff, was her escort that gorgeous sunny day. I'm sure the crown *never* looked as beautiful on anyone's head as it did shining above her long, softly curled dark hair. I leaned over and said, "Marilyn, honey, last night before they announced your name as the winner, did you have any idea you'd be queen?"

I'll never forget how she turned to me and quietly and deliberately said, "Yes, Joyce, I knew a few minutes before they announced it."

I thought so! She hadn't looked a bit surprised when they put the crown on her head.

"How did you know?" I questioned. "You really knew?"

"Yes, and I'll tell you why. Three weeks ago, during my devotions, the Lord asked me if I would give up something. [She never told me *what* it was other than that it was something very special to her.] I told the Lord 'yes.' Then He showed me something else and

133

asked the same question and I swallowed hard, but said, 'Yes.' Then He asked me to give up a third thing, only this was something I *really* loved, so it took a little longer, but in the end I said, 'Yes, Lord, even that.'

"Then, ever so quietly, the Lord said, 'Marilyn, three times I've tested you by asking you to give up something and three times you've *willingly* said yes. Now, I'm going to give you three yes's back.'

"Two weeks later the representative from the freshman class formally asked me to be one of the twelve girls competing for homecoming queen. The Lord said at the end of that day, 'That was your first yes.'

"One week after that I was chosen one of the five finalists. The Lord said, 'That was your second yes.'

"The night of the crowning none of us knew who would be queen, but we were all waiting for the master of ceremonies to announce the winner. I was in line on the stage with the other girls when I heard the Lord clearly say, 'Marilyn, I'm about to give you your third yes.' I knew what He was going to do."

She had claimed nothing. She had even been willing to lose three very dear things, and because of that God bestowed a delightful honor on her

Marilyn is rich, you see, in *trusting* and *obeying*. It's really hard for some of us to remember that most of God's promises to us depend on those two words. It's quite an exchange! We give Him trust and obedience; He gives riches and treasures *beyond* our hope. Marilyn gave Him those two qualities and He rewarded her with a remarkable inner wealth.

She has told me the exact circumstances in which she gave her whole life to the Lord. It was just hours after our mother's funeral. Marilyn was fourteen, frightened, and unbelievably hurt and bewildered by mother's death.

Friends and relatives had left. I'd gone home with my family; my brother, Cliff, had taken a military jet back to Vietnam; and my father had wearily gone to bed.

She went into the den and, realizing her aloneness, asked God to be her Friend, Savior, and Comforter. In short, she did an incredible thing — *she forgave* the Lord for taking her mother. He, in turn, melted the hurt and bitterness and began to heal her torn heart. In those moments she started to become the beautiful, wealthy person we love.

When I think of her, at such a young age forgiving the Lord for mother's death, I remember the widow who said angrily to me, "Just how am I supposed to be thankful for my husband's death two years ago?"

I told her she'd *never* get over that death until she could get to the bottom of the problem. There she stood, some two years after her husband's death, still shaking her fist in God's face demanding to know why He had done this terrible thing to her. She will always be spiritually poor until the lesson of forgiveness melts her hardened heart and begins its healing.

Marilyn is rich because her forgiveness is always up-to-date. She's determined to be the woman God wants her to be.

Another millionaire friend is Sheila. Knowing her has been (and is) a profitable experience. She continually adds to my wealth. Several years ago Dick asked me if I needed someone to help with my house-cleaning. I glanced at my desk, took a long look at the stack of letters to be answered, and put into words what had been just a vague idea.

"You know, a housekeeper isn't what I need. I desperately have to have a secretary." I almost surprised myself because I'd never really thought about one — how much I would need one, how I'd find one, or even how much it would cost. Yet there I stood, realizing that as I checked my mental priority list the top line said, "Secretary — now!"

That night Dick and I earnestly prayed about a secretary. "Lord," I said, "You know I don't have the faintest idea if I even need a secretary really, except for someone to answer the mail. (I hadn't written my first book, *Let's Have a Banquet,* yet.) I don't know where to find a secretary or how much I'd need one each week, but it seems clear that I should talk to You about it."

Then Dick prayed, "Send us a secretary, Lord." He's more direct and takes business-like shortcuts.

The next morning the phone rang. It was Sheila. She is from our church, and before her first baby came along she was an executive secretary. She was calling me about some church matter and stopped mid-sentence to say, "Oh, maybe you're busy, and I should call back later."

"Oh, no," I answered, "I'm just sitting here at my desk answering fifty letters from radio listeners." At that time I had a daily syndicated radio show, and the mail response was somewhat overwhelming.

136

"Why don't you let me help you with them?" she asked.

"Oh, no," I laughed. "I don't want to bother anybody with. . . ." *What am I saying?* I thought. *Here I prayed last night for the Lord to send me a secretary, and I was on the phone saying, "oh, no," to a gal who had been a top executive's brains for four years!*

As my head cleared a little I heard Sheila's voice sweetly saying, "I've been praying ever since Darin was born that the Lord would let me use my typing and shorthand on a part-time basis so I wouldn't lose my touch or skills."

I pulled myself together and asked, "Would you be my secretary?"

"Yes, I'd love to," came the answer.

Since her forgiveness is complete in the Lord, she is totally free to accept her life. She went from executive secretary to wife, mother, and homemaker with joy. Nothing was lost in the transition, yet the Lord had given her the brains to develop her natural secretarial skills, and when the timing was right He provided the exact outlet she needed. Those skills were sharpened and kept alive. She handles both her household and secretarial jobs with ever growing success.

The only disagreement we've had in three years is: did the Lord answer *my* prayer or Sheila's? (I say *mine!*)

This Thanksgiving she made me rich again by a short note delivered through our son, Rick. She didn't come in, just handed it to him with, "Here, give this to your mother."

The note said:

"Happy Thanksgiving!

"I decided you're due for a note, so here's my Thanksgiving list for you:

"I'm thankful for you . . .

"1. Because nearly every time we talk you leave me with some new, lovely, strengthening, or growth-producing thought to ponder.

"2. Because sometimes you sing a song for me — just me. I thought all day about the one, 'I was in His mind.' Then the Lord gave me the verse to go with it, Ephesians 1:4.

"3. Because I learn so much from the things I type.

"4. Because you must be the classiest person I know, yet the only one I know who wears bobby sox with her flats. You make me laugh. . . . [Come on, Sheila, it was cold that day!]

"5. Because I'm so proud to say, 'Thank you. Joyce *made* it or *gave* it to me.'

"6. Because you bring such pretty flowers to brighten my day.

"7. Because it's fun to come to your house and enjoy your friends — that's why I'm so quiet. I'm enjoying everyone's conversation.

"8. Because I loved chapter one of *The Richest Lady in Town*. All right — you may well *be* the richest lady in town, but I'm wealthy too because I have the Lord *and* you!"

The next time you think you have to spend a fortune on a gift for a friend, remember Sheila's priceless letter to me and write your own to someone you love. It will be much more impressive than an expensive gift elegantly wrapped, and it will last forever!

I have been made wealthy by the strength of character, surrender, and ministry I see in another friend. Her name is Ruth.

Ruth has writing talent — I mean real, gifted writing ability. It's a deep source of wealth to me.

For years many people have sent or given me their writings — songs, poems, articles, and books. I've looked at all of them. Some are great, some are incredibly bad, some are just routine, even a little boring; but I've enjoyed even the bad ones because the people took time to write their thoughts down on paper. (Millions of sincere men and women say they are going to write a book, but very few really do.)

But Ruth's writing always takes my breath away! Whether it is a serious letter, a thank-you note, a prayer, a poem, a song, or whatever, it always really affects me and it takes a while to recover! Her writings continually speak to me.

A friend once said, "Ruth's thank-you notes are the only ones in the world that require writing a thank-you back!"

Her letters to hundreds of people during the years have given great joy. Her Christmas gift to me last December was truly rare. No other gift gave me so much.

It was a folder of "mini-mood" thoughts. The front page read,

"Dear, dear Joyce:
"One day at the beauty shop you asked if I had been

139

writing. I told you no, because there was no other true answer. However, I have — from time to time — been jotting down 'mini-moods.' Little bits of prayer and reflection that have suddenly just 'been there.'

"You would laugh if you could see the scraps of paper and envelopes and registration cards and corners of grocery sacks I had to gather together in order to type these for you, but somehow I wanted so much to do it!

"Perhaps you'll remember that several years ago I gave you the story of Sam for your birthday — along with other story outlines. That memory keeps coming back to me this Christmas season. And again, I'm suddenly overwhelmed with a sort of ache to share something with you not found at a store counter — something that says, 'I am Ruth and I want very much to give part of me away to Joyce this Christmas.' The reason is simple: Just my gratitude and love.

"So here is my special, personal gift to you. Out of many moods I have chosen these few with tender loving care!

"May your Christmas be —

All Joy!
Ruth"

Of all the mini-moods this one was my favorite. It was called,

WHO WILL CLAP FOR ME?

I am often dramatic
Sometimes ecstatic
In the role I play

On the stage of Life
I bow
And smile
And bask
In the limelight,
Hoarding each moment
Of thunderous applause,
But when the curtain is pulled
For the last time,
When the crowds have dispersed
And the stage is dark,
Who will clap for me then, Lord?
You?

Ruth's writing, particularly in the last years, has a rare freshness. Now if this was all there was to her wealth, you might be asking, "So she's talented, that's nice. So what?"

Just this. Every time I read something of Ruth's I think, *Wow, I wish I'd written that,* or *I wish the Lord would have said that through me.* In short, I wish I had her talent. However, I'm not sure that if I had her talent I'd still be writing. Although God has given Ruth a truly gifted mind which expresses itself through her writings, very few of them have been published, and you may never, except here, read any of them.

I would have quit writing long, long ago. I would have broken every pencil in half and confined my writing to postcards saying, "Having a wonderful time. Wish you were here."

Ruth has every right to do one of two things; get

141

mad and quit or become bitter and blame God for not opening a publisher's door for her. Yet she remains obedient to what she knows God wants her to do which is, *write*. Sure, she's had some things published, but not nearly what could have been.

Actually to Ruth, whether or not she will be published is not really a big deal. She has been given a ministry which, for now at least, means writing just to individuals. It is unique and without visible fame or financial rewards, yet her wealth is enormous! She is steeped in the fragrance of forgiveness.

I am one of the hundreds of people she will write to this year. Her direct contact with the Lord and the gift of expressing on paper what is needed is phenomenal. It may be a quick poem in the center of the page or a long detailed letter, but it always arrives at the right time and meets the precise need. Over and over again I'm enriched by Ruth as she continues to let the Holy Spirit lead her. You may never see a book of hers for sale at a bookstore, but in heaven's library the card file clearly indicates, *Ruth is published.*

Another friend I'd like you to meet is an Army chaplain's wife named Carolyn. To me she is the epitome of the beatitude that says, "Happy are the utterly sincere, for they will see God" (Matt. 5:8, Phillips' translation).

Carolyn is completely honest with herself, her husband, family, friends, and above all, God. In honesty I must tell you that she has forgiven the U. S. Government, the Pentagon, the Army, and the Military Chaplains' Corps. I've never heard her complain about military life.

Colleen Evans wrote unknowingly of my friend, Carolyn, when she described the "utterly sincere" as ". . . the woman who gives every conscious area of her life to God, and goes on to ask Him to reveal areas of the subconscious that need to be healed and given over. There is no inner tension in this woman, for she seeks to hide nothing from God or man."

Carolyn lives her life as the wife of a military man in that kind of honesty, and consequently she reveals no inner tensions. In fact, one of her loveliest traits is a well-developed, marvelous sense of humor. She is such a comedienne she makes me smile, giggle, and down-right howl, yet I have wept with her in prayerful moments. Having a sense of humor really boils down to this fact; you don't take yourself *dead* seriously. What happens to you, big events or small annoyances, are not really of earth-shaking importance in the light of Peking or the atomic bomb. But this kind of evaluating takes honesty.

Carolyn is also one of the few women I know who acts her age without sobbing about it. She doesn't try to be some young chick but has *accepted* her age. That may not sound like any big deal to you, but, from all the conversations I've heard at women's meetings, age is one thing *very* few women have on their "most wanted" list. Carolyn, with a married daughter and a teen-age son, has adopted the attitude that she is exactly the age God wants her to be — not a moment older and not a moment younger. Growing older is never a threat to the woman who is securely loved by Christ.

When I did the last two military tours for the Chap-

143

lains' Division in the Far East, I needed the rich gifts that Carolyn so lovingly gave to me in Okinawa. One was the gift of laughter, and believe me, with 35 performances to 8,000 people in 21 days of touring, I *needed* a laugh. The other gift was that honesty that freed her from inner tensions. She refreshed my weary spirit in a hundred ways with these two gifts, and, even though I'm home now, the gifts still creep into my memory at odd times, and I smile because I'm blessed and warmed all over again!

This last millionaire friend, Mary, is the wealthiest woman I know.

When I was overseas singing and speaking for the Army chaplains this year, Mary wrote a letter to my children. It was a beautiful letter thanking them for letting me go so far away, and it ended with many encouraging words to keep them from getting too lonely.

That understanding, warm letter was the *only* one my children received although there were literally hundreds of people who knew I'd be gone. Mary, and Mary alone, had the foresight and insight to write. It was a most priceless gift to me, but it was even more priceless and precious to Rick and Laurie as they know Mary is paralyzed from the neck down, and a handwritten letter from her involves a superhuman amount of effort!

Fifteen years ago, Mary was stricken with both spinal and bulbar forms of poliomyelitis. That she survived was only one of God's miracles. That her young minister husband, Keith, stayed by her side through the long thirteen months she lived, no, existed

144

in the iron lung was equally spectacular. There were sixteen women in Mary's ward who had been stricken with polio that year. Almost all of their marriages dissolved. Some husbands never again showed up in the hospital once the doctors had given the diagnosis of polio.

Mary, Keith, and their two little children, Ken and Karen, began living in a completely different manner. Their lives would never be as they had once planned.

When Mary was finally able to emerge from the iron lung she came home — but came home to begin life completely paralyzed, to take up life as a wife and mother without any ability to move, sit, or walk.

It was soon after she arrived from the hospital that the truth of how her life would now be really hit Keith. Their little girl, Karen, two-and-a-half years old, had fallen down while playing outside. Karen did what all children do — she ran to her mommy, sobbing and holding up her skinned knee.

Keith's mind and eyes photographed the scene indelibly. He watched as Mary, in shocked silence, realized she could not pick Karen up. She could not bend over her, hug her, or kiss her hurt away. She could not lift Karen and comfort the sobbing child. In fact, she *never* even would be able to do the routine, normal, almost everyday thing required of mothers with children and skinned knees, the hugging, the holding, and the kissing — a privilege I've taken for granted most of my life as a mother. The scene shattered Keith's heart and he wondered how they'd ever pull themselves together. However, he was soon to find that a new Mary would emerge — quiet but incredibly strong.

145

It must have been here, during the early days of the tragedy, that Mary did some exploratory surgery deep within her own soul. I do not imagine that it was easy.

You and I, faced with the same set of circumstances might not have been able to do what Mary did, but somehow she managed to lay her stiffened body in the arms of God, and in those moments the Mary her friends might never have seen began to emerge. Had it not been for the tragic disease called polio, we might have missed this amazing woman.

I believe this beautiful life came into its own when she forgave God. The anger and bitterness was replaced by a quiet, peaceful joy and springing up came a well of wisdom so rare I'm always stunned by it.

Both Keith and Mary have taken this tragedy, this bitterly hard turn of events, and for sixteen years have turned it, daily, over to God. It has never been easy, and it has never been fun, and their life has *not* been what they dreamed about as young lovers. Yet, what they have is so much more! Their wealth is enormous! Having lived through these years they have known, seen, and experienced dimensions of God that few people in an entire lifetime will ever see. I think it's interesting to note that when my heart is breaking, I call them. When I need direction about my children, I call them. When I'm faced with a difficult decision, I call them. When I need objective thinking, I call them. Why? Because they are the biggest bank of help I've ever known. They have enormous holdings in trust, great wealth in obedience, and in the face of insurmountable odds, they are rich in praise of our Lord.

Because their ability to forgive is so clearly established, they are freed to be the people God wants them to be. Mary's gentle faith continues to smother out the flames of self-centered resentment.

They have survived one crisis after another, from Mary, just this past year, being temporarily returned to an iron lung to the almost constant search for *another* nurse/housekeeper combination.

In the years I've known Mary, the closest I've heard her come to complaining was one day when she said wistfully, "Just sometimes, I wish I could pick up my toothbrush and brush my own teeth." (Another privilege I've taken for granted all my life!)

Mary and Keith know more about the words "flexibility" and "adjustment" than any other people I've ever met. Polio has been a refining element in their lives and they have come forth as gold!

Just yesterday, as Keith sat across from me in our living room, his face wet with tears, he spoke tenderly and glowingly of his quiet Mary. "I've said it publicly," he said "and it sounds so editorial. We ministers get like that sometimes — yet it's true. Mary, very soon after polio struck, began to show and exhibit an amazing strength. This quiet, soft-spoken woman's character began to emerge as a towering strength, and not only that, but she was given a most beautiful child-like faith that in these years has been utterly unshakable!"

Then today a note came from Keith. He wrote of her faith, "She doesn't talk in golden glowing phrases about it . . . that's not her gift. She just *lives* it! And how she enriches my life. The tenderness and gentle-

ness that I believe God has brought to my ministry, He
has given *through Mary!*"

They have lived with the deep sorrow and desperate
disappointment of Mary's illness (although they never
speak of it as such) with so much nerve and courage
that whenever I read, "How happy are those who
know what sorrow means, for they will be given courage and comfort!" (Matt. 5:4, Phillips' translation), I
think of *them.*

Mary and Keith have seen in their lifetime the death
of a whole way of life they thought they'd have, yet
they are happy in the secure knowledge that God continues to control every facet of their living. It is He
who has helped Mary master the art of staying alive.
It is His power that has given her such strong will-
power. The doctors are incredulous that the atrophied
leg muscles can take slow, stiff, but sure steps. It is
His courage that helps her endure and adapt to the
braces and captive metal fittings that give her some
measure of control over lifeless arms and legs. She
never loses sight of the hope God has given her, and
because of that beautiful, shining hope within her, she
is my richest friend!

These millionaire friends all have one thing in common in their lives: forgiveness — acceptance of God's
forgiveness and an ability to forgive others. That's
how they opened their accounts in the Bank of Heaven.

Just think! If you know Christ, if He has forgiven
you your sin and you have asked Him to live inside
you, you, too, have the Bank of Heaven at your service.
You have at least one priceless gift, the one of eternal,

everlasting life. If you stopped right there you'd be far wealthier than many people, but *don't* stop there.

Christ came to give us eternal life in the future, *but* He also came to give us abundant life right here and now, a life that overflows with riches — even if your name is Mary and your body is paralyzed, because your mind and spirit are free to move, expand, develop, and overflow with life.

I spoke at a mother-and-daughter banquet about the need for God's forgiveness in our lives and our need to forgive others. Many months later the pastor's wife told me she had left that banquet just glowing because she was so certain her forgiveness was all taken care of. She took her children home and then drove back to the church to help the clean-up crews. As she cleaned she was congratulating herself on being so spiritually right, when suddenly she heard the Lord say, "What about your mother-in-law?"

"Oh, that," she responded. "Well, I've forgiven her, Lord, you know that!"

"Then why do you talk about her the way you do?" the Lord quietly questioned.

She realized that every time anyone related an awful-thing-my-mother-in-law-did story, she topped it with one about her mother-in-law that was bigger and better.

The Lord brought such conviction that night that she asked His and her mother-in-law's forgiveness and she has lived and coped with the problem ever since. She is free really to love that mother-in-law and to keep still when others talk about their mothers-in-law.

That's a small issue compared with Mary's illness,

149

but both women have learned the lesson of forgiveness. You can too.

Right now, remember that if you have asked God to forgive you, *He has.* He promised that He would and He cannot lie, so if you've asked, He has heard and *done it!*

Now, accept it. Stop hemming and hawing around. It's free. Take it. Don't remind God of how awful or undeserving you are or what awful sins you have committed. You're wasting your time. He already knows all about you and is still ready to forgive, so accept it. It's yours.

That will free you to *forgive* others of anything. It will also free you to *accept* others as they are without trying to make them into your image. But most of all it will allow you truly to *love* others. Even circumstances can be forgiven, accepted, and loved under these conditions.

You can spend your life paralyzed, not by polio, but by bitterness, anger, even apathy, or an unforgiving spirit.

But that's such a waste — the Lord waits with vast accounts called forgiveness and healing and your name is marked as owner.

So, with all this in mind, climb out of that rut of hopelessness. Stop sitting in the chair marked "poor me." Stop looking at your picture albums of past failures. Don't let the hideous infection of bitterness and anger keep your wounds from a complete healing. Stop nagging the Lord about the "whys?" of your problems and put down those large boxes of worry and fear — you don't need to carry them around!

You have a great God! You were born to live life with all its exciting peculiarities and its stressing, tension-filled problems. God knows your tolerance quota. He won't bend you past the breaking point. Furthermore, when you were born the second time, you were automatically born into the great kingdom of God. The King is your Father! Your rights, your inheritance and your access to Him are yours because *you belong to Him. You are His child, His heir!* Think of it — your Father is the King!

Paul's prayer in Colossians 2 is my prayer for you. Every time I read it, a happy, clanging bell starts to ring inside me.

> This is what I have asked of God for you: that you will be encouraged and knit together by strong ties of love, and that you will have the *rich* experience of knowing *Christ* with real certainty and clear understanding. *For God's secret plan, now at last made known, is Christ himself.*
>
> In him lie hidden all the mighty, untapped *treasures* of wisdom and knowledge.
>
> I am saying this because I am afraid that someone may fool you with smooth talk. For though I am far away from you my heart is with you, happy because you are getting along so well, happy because of your strong faith in Christ. And now just as you trusted Christ to save you, trust him, too, for each day's problems; live in vital union with him. Let your roots grow down into him and draw up nourishment from him. See that you go on growing in the Lord, and become strong and vigorous in the truth you were taught. Let your lives overflow with joy and thanksgiving for all he has done.

151

Don't let others spoil your faith and joy with their philosophies, their wrong and shallow answers built on men's thoughts and ideas, instead of on what Christ has said. For in Christ there is all of God in a human body; *so you have everything when you have Christ,* and you are filled with God through your union with Christ. He is the highest Ruler, with authority over every other power (Col. 2:2-10, *Living Bible*).

Did that really get through to you? Can you grab that fantastic, basic truth and live it? *"You have everything when you have Christ!"*

Just this morning, as I was reading Corinthians, one verse jumped out at me. It said,

"You know how full of love and kindness our Lord Jesus was: though he was so very rich, yet to help you he became so very poor, so that by being poor he could make you rich" (2 Cor. 8:9, *Living Bible*).

How rich He was! Yet He gave it up, and through His sacrifice, *we were made rich!*

It's time you woke up each morning realizing it — it's time you knew it and acted on it, especially if things are going all wrong for you. It's so true — you do have *everything* when you have Him!

It's really about time you threw open the shutters of your heart, pulled out all the stops on your vocal chords, and yelled to the neighbors next door, the people uptown and downtown, and to the whole world in general — "Hey, look at *me.* I have everything, and praise the Lord, you know what? *I'm* the richest lady in town!

"That's right, *me!*

"*I'm* the richest lady in town!"